THE EPISTLES OF

ST. CLEMENT OF ROME

AND

ST. IGNATIUS OF ANTIOCH

Ancient Christian Writers

THE WORKS OF THE FATHERS IN TRANSLATION

EDITED BY

JOHANNES QUASTEN, S. T. D.
Professor of Ancient Church History and Christian Archaeology

JOSEPH C. PLUMPE, Ph. D.
Professor of New Testament Greek and Ecclesiastical Latin

The Catholic University of America
Washington, D. C.

No. 1

THE EPISTLES OF
ST. CLEMENT OF ROME
AND
ST. IGNATIUS OF ANTIOCH

NEWLY TRANSLATED AND ANNOTATED

BY

JAMES A. KLEIST, S.J., Ph.D.

Professor of Classical Languages
St. Louis University
St. Louis, Mo.

PAULIST PRESS
New York / Mahwah

Imprimi Potest:

Joseph P Zuercher, S.J.
Provincialis
S. Ludovici, Mo., die 5 Aprilis 1946

Nihil Obstat:

Johannes Quasten, S.T.D.
Censor Deputatus

Imprimatur:

Michael J. Curley, D.D.
Archiepiscopus Baltimorensis et Washingtonensis
die 11 Maii 1946

Library of Congress
Catalog Card Number: 78-62448

ISBN: 0-8091-0038-X

PUBLISHED BY PAULIST PRESS
997 Macarthur Blvd.
Mahwah, NJ 07430

PRINTED AND BOUND IN THE UNITED STATES OF AMERICA

FOREWORD BY THE EDITORS

The present volume marks the inauguration of ANCIENT CHRISTIAN WRITERS. This series addresses itself to all who remain conscious of a most precious ancient heritage, the works of the Fathers; and it purposes to make these works available in a new English translation that is at once faithful to the original message and intelligible to the reader of our century.

That there is need of such a new collection of translations should be evident. On the Catholic side we have been entirely without one for much too long. So far back as 1941 the editors on their walks through the Maryland fields and woods discussed this situation and determined to devote every effort to its correction. Plainly, though, their first efforts needed to be given to the enlistment of collaborators, of a corps of scholars in whom there would be certain warranty that the great task of translating the patristic literature would be done competently. The task of engaging a responsible publisher was an easier one: Mr. William Eckenrode, Director of Newman Bookshop, Westminster, Maryland, responded most generously and enthusiastically. But to the great satisfaction of the editors the invitations to their colleagues throughout the English-speaking world also were heartily received. Acceptances came in great number from scholars in America, England, Ireland, and Australia, from men who are specialists in the wide patristic field and are now engaged in translating.

Thus only, if competent scholars here and abroad were approached, could there be any hope that the series would include the Greek and Latin Fathers and also give all due consideration to the Christian Oriental sources—so much neglected in the past—be they of Armenian, Arabic, Syriac, or Coptic provenience. The collection, then, will offer many texts that up to now have not appeared in English version and which in part have been discovered only in recent decades.

Since in any good translation of patristic literature philological precision must go hand in hand with theological understanding, the new collection sets itself the task of meeting both requirements. To this end, too, the editors are giving due attention to the primary requisite of basing all translations on the most recent and trustworthy editions of the ancient texts. They are, moreover, keenly aware of the great difficulties that all too frequently confront the good translator, who would be both scrupulously loyal to the ancient wording and most considerate of the modern reader's moods and tastes. But at the same time they are firmly convinced that in no case do the two ends postulate a cleavage that calls for too great concessions one way or the other. There must always be a happy *via media*, passable to the exacting scholar and to the discerning layman; though to the translator there is a challenge: *hic patet ingeniis campus.*

The history of mankind has recorded no more momentous event than the founding of Christianity. The Fathers of the Church are eyewitnesses to the gradual growth and expansion of the new religion, as they were, and remain, witnesses to the faith transmitted to us from their times. Their written reports accompany the development of the Church throughout her youth, from the Apostolic times through the period of persecution and into the glorious day of Christianity's triumph over the ancient paganism. A world enmeshed in superstition and materialism was conquered for the Imperator Christ. Victory—of this Christianity in the flush of its youth is indubitably confident and absolutely certain; and this is the characteristic note of all the works of the Fathers, whether they wrote them out of the vibrant enthusiasm of their stout hearts or penned them under the restraint of less sanguine natures, whether they were masters of rhetoric or given to abstract contemplation, whether they moved in the world as princes of the Church or fled it to spend their days as desèrt solitaries. Consciousness of victory animated them all, the Christian slave girl and martyr Blandina no less than Tertullian or Lactantius. Thus the entire patristic literature bears the stamp of victorious combat. It is for this reason that the editors have chosen for ANCIENT CHRISTIAN WRITERS a seal that gives expression to this outlook of confidence, in the early Christian acclamation:

IHCOYC XPICTOC NIKA
JESUS CHRIST CONQUERS!

J. Q.
J. C. P.

Feast of St. Athanasius, 1946.

CONTENTS

ST. CLEMENT OF ROME
THE EPISTLE TO THE CORINTHIANS

INTRODUCTION

Clement and Ignatius belong to that group of ancient Christian writers known as the *Apostolic Fathers*—a term of comparatively recent origin and meant to signify that these writers had, or were supposed to have had, some personal contact with the Apostles.[1]

St. Clement's *Epistle to the Corinthians* purports to be addressed by "the Church of Rome" to "the Church of Corinth." The writer's name is not mentioned in it; nevertheless, the Clementine authorship was not doubted in antiquity and has been called in question in modern times on but slender grounds.[2] Eusebius and St. Jerome state that it was written by Clement "as a representative (ἐν προσώπῳ) of the Church of Rome." According to some critics the author was the third, according to others, the second, successor to St. Peter. St. Epiphanius relates that he was indeed ordained by the latter, but for the sake of peace made room for Linus to follow the Apostle in the episcopacy. His own term of office must have fallen somewhere between the years 92 and 101. The persecution mentioned at the beginning of the letter was not the Neronian, but that set on foot by Domitian. That Clement was of Jewish parentage is plausibly inferred from his fondness for drawing heavily upon the Old Testament for illustrative material. He has been identified by some with St. Paul's fellow laborer of the same name, mentioned in Phil. 4.3. His namesake, Clement of Alexandria, and others thought so highly of his letter that they included it

3

in the canon of the New Testament. Neither the place nor the manner of his death is known. The Latin Church keeps his feast on November 23. All our information regarding Clement, such as it is, is due to notices by St. Irenaeus, Tertullian, Dionysius of Corinth, Hegesippus, Clement of Alexandria, Origen, Eusebius, St. Epiphanius, and St. Jerome.

The *Epistle to the Corinthians* here presented is called " the first epistle " in contradistinction to a second, which is held to be spurious. It is generally supposed to have been written about 96, and is, therefore, prior to the letters of Ignatius. Of the many points of difference between the two productions, the most notable is that Ignatius wrote as a friend to friends, in a personal affair and in a cordial manner, though not without occasional sharp denunciations of certain heretical teachers. The tone of the Clementine epistle, on the other hand, is that proper to an outspoken, firm, yet fatherly, reprimand administered to an entire con-gregation. A delegation of prominent Roman Christians brought the letter to Corinth, and Clement emphatically indicates that he expects a speedy and satisfactory answer. There is no time allowed for parleying; what is expected is outright submission. Now, because Clement speaks " as the representative of the Roman Church " and assumes the right to interfere in the internal affairs of another Church, Catholics are inclined to see in the epistle an *actual* proof of their belief that even at that early date the Bishop of Rome was regarded as the head of the universal Church. There is no explicit expression in the letter of the primacy of the bishop of Rome, yet neither is there anything in it to clash with this belief.

The occasion for this epistle was furnished by the rebellious conduct of some members of the Corinthian community, who had taken upon themselves to depose several officials of the Church in defiance of ecclesiastical authority. By far the greater part of the community was drawn into this " unholy and detestable schism," which was a scandal even to their pagan neighbors. The news of it reached Rome, and Rome interfered. That Clement's endeavor to restore order was successful seems clear from a statement made by a later bishop of Corinth, Dionysius, in a letter to Pope Soter (about 170), that Clement's epistle, together with Soter's own letter, was being read at church assemblies.

The epistle is a model of a pastoral letter. "With great tact and mature insight into human character, with gentle forbearance and yet deep earnestness, Clement accomplished the delicate task that devolved on him because of the situation at Corinth." [8] He draws an impressive picture of the conduct of a true Christian, so that his epistle is in reality a homily on Christian life. After portraying in vivid colors the once flourishing condition of the Corinthian Church (chs. 1 and 2), Clement goes straight to the heart of the matter and points out that the cause of the schism was the " jealousy and envy " of a few " rash and headstrong individuals." He then launches into a comprehensive survey of ancient Jewish and contemporary Christian history to show that all disturbances in the past were due to " jealousy and envy," while all blessings ever were, and always will be, attendant upon the preservation of peace and concord among men, and, above all, upon submission to authority. Order, he holds, is the expression of the will of God; disorder, the seed sown by the Prince of this world. This is the theme of Part I (chs. 3-36). Then, alluding to a soldier's obedience to his commanders, he passes on to Part II (37-61) with this exhortation: " Let us, then, brethren, do soldier's duty in downright earnest under the banner of His (Christ's) glorious commands." He now concerns himself with the special disorder existing in the Corinthian community, and in strong, yet restrained, language emphasizes the need of the spirit of submissiveness. He urgently calls upon the authors of the schism to lay aside their ambitious schemes and repent. Chapters 62-65 recapitulate the theme of the epistle and express the confident hope that his fatherly admonitions will not be lost upon the Church of Corinth.

After grappling with the linguistic problems of the Ignatian letters, a translator breathes more freely when he turns to Clement's epistle and finds in it something of the ancient gracefulness of diction. Clement was doubtless an educated Roman and conversant with the requirements of good prose style. Not that his diction is couched in classical Greek, though this has been affirmed by one or two critics; still, in contrast with Ignatius's display of passion and individuality, Clement masters his feelings and presents his thoughts in smooth and balanced form. His appeal is to the reason and sound judgment of his readers. It should be noted, however, that his rather lengthy quotations from the Old Testament do not always tally with our standard text of the Septuagint, and that, besides, he has a way of blending statements made by different writers on different occasions, with the result that there are not a few obscurities in his exposition that defy precise interpretation.

Clement's epistle was highly prized in antiquity. It is a pleasure, though no surprise, to note that Clement and Ignatius agree on all essential matters. Both are strong witnesses to the Church's monarchical form of government. The officials of the Church are generally referred to by Clement as ἐπίσκοποι καὶ διάκονοι; in one passage (44.5), they are styled πρεσβύτεροι. The terminology was still fluid at the time, and had not yet acquired that precision which we meet in later Christian literature. Another point of agreement is that, just as Ignatius takes for granted that the Church has "one altar" (ἓν θυσιαστήριον) and, consequently, one "sacrifice," so Clement describes the chief function of Church officials as that of " offering the gifts of the faithful " (προσφέροντες τὰ δῶρα). The solemn liturgical prayer of thanksgiving in 59.4-61.3 attests the belief of the Roman Church in the divine nature of Jesus—a point never lost sight of in the theology of Ignatius. Significant, too, is Clement's assertion that Church officials do not derive their authority from the people, but from God. Such, too, is Ignatius's view. Incidentally, we learn from Clement that St. Peter sojourned at Rome (ἐν ἡμῖν), and that St. Paul visited Spain (τὸ τέρμα τῆς δύσεως).

It is important for the modern Christian reader to realize that Clement, representing the Occident, and Ignatius, representing the Orient, are in agreement regarding the form of Christianity which they profess. The Christian Church shows the same face, whether seen through the eyes of Clement, or those of Ignatius. Both are convinced, too, that this form corresponds to the Apostolic tradition, which, in their minds, is in complete harmony with Scripture. The same is true of the rest of the Apostolic Fathers. Under such circumstances, is it any wonder that the Council of Trent requires Catholic theologians to interpret Scripture "according to the unanimous consent of the Fathers "?

In conclusion it may be mentioned that a considerable pseudo-Clementine literature grew up in course of time. Whatever other value these writings may have, one incidental value is that they testify to the high esteem which St. Clement, Bishop of Rome, enjoyed in antiquity.

❧　❧　❧

The text used for this translation is that of F. X. Funk, revised by K. Bihlmeyer, *Die Apostolischen Väter*, 1. Teil (Tübingen 1924).

Other modern translations are contained in the following works, some of them referred to in the Notes:

Knopf, R., *Die Lehre der zwölf Apostel. Die zwei Klemensbriefe* (Handbuch zum Neuen Testament, Ergänzungsb.: Die Apostolischen Väter 1-3, Tübingen 1920).

Knopf, R.–Krüger, G., in E. Hennecke's *Neutestamentliche Apokryphen* (2d ed., Tübingen 1924) 482-502.

Lake, K., *The Apostolic Fathers* 1 (Loeb Classical Library, London 1930).

Lightfoot, J. B., *The Apostolic Fathers. Part 1: S. Clement of Rome* 2 (London 1890).

Zeller, F., *Die Apostolischen Väter* (Bibliothek der Kirchenväter, 2d ed., Kempten-Munich 1918).

THE FIRST EPISTLE OF CLEMENT
TO THE CORINTHIANS [1]

The Church of God which resides as a stranger at Rome [2] to the Church of God which is a stranger at Corinth; to those who are called and sanctified [3] by the will of God through [4] our Lord Jesus Christ. May grace and peace from Almighty God flow to you in rich profusion through Jesus Christ!

1. Owing to the suddenly bursting and rapidly succeeding calamities and untoward experiences [5] that have befallen us, we have been somewhat tardy, we think, in giving our attention to the subjects of dispute [6] in your community, beloved. We mean that execrable and godless schism so utterly foreign to the elect of God. And it is only a few rash and headstrong individuals that have inflamed it to such a degree of madness that your venerable, widely-renowned, and universally and deservedly cherished name has been greatly defamed. 2 Indeed, was there ever a visitor in your midst that did not approve your excellent and steadfast faith? Or did not admire your discreet and thoughtful [7] Christian piety? Or did not proclaim the magnificent character of your hospitality? Or did not congratulate you on your perfect and secure fund of knowledge? [8] 3 You certainly did everything without an eye to rank or station in life, and regulated your conduct by God's commandments. You were submissive to your officials and paid the older men among you the respect due to them. The young you trained to habits of

self-restraint and sedateness. The wives you enjoined to discharge all their duties with a conscience pure and undefiled,
and to cherish a dutiful affection for their husbands; you
taught them also to stay within the established norm of
obedience in managing the household with decency and
consummate prudence.[9]

2. Moreover, you were all in a humble frame of mind, in
no way arrogant, practicing obedience rather than demanding
it, happier in giving than in receiving.[10] Being content with,
and intent upon, the provisions [11] which Christ allowed you
for your earthly pilgrimage, it was His words that you care-
fully locked up in your hearts, and His sufferings were ever
before your eyes. 2 Thus all were blessed with a profound
and radiant peace of soul, and there was an insatiable longing
to do good, as well as a rich outpouring of the Holy Spirit
upon the whole community.[12] 3 Filled, moreover, with a
desire for holiness, you stretched out your hands, with ready
goodwill and devout confidence, to Almighty God, imploring
Him to show mercy in case you had inadvertently failed in
any way. 4 Day and night you vied with one another in
behalf of the entire brotherhood,[13] to further the salvation of
the full number of His elect by your compassion and con-
scientiousness. 5 Guileless and sincere you were, and bore
one another no malice. 6 The very thought of insubordination and schism was an abomination to you. Over the failings
of your neighbors you mourned; their shortcomings you
judged to be your own. 7 You had no regrets when you had
been charitable, *being ready for any good deed.*[14] 8 Decked
with the jewel of a virtuous life that commanded veneration,
you fulfilled all your duties in the fear of the Lord, whose
precepts and ordinances were engraved upon the tablets of
your heart.[15]

3. All splendor and scope for expansion were bestowed upon you, and then the Scripture was fulfilled: [16] *The beloved ate and drank, and he waxed large and fat, and then he kicked out.* 2 From this sprang jealousy and envy, strife and sedition, persecution and anarchy, war and captivity. 3 Then *the dishonored* rose up *against the honored,*[17] the ignoble against the highly esteemed, the foolish against the wise, the young against their elders. 4 For this reason piety and peace are far removed, because everyone has abandoned the fear of God and lost the clear vision which faith affords, and nobody regulates his conduct by the norms of His commandments, or tries to make his life worthy of Christ. On the contrary, everyone follows the appetites of his depraved heart, for they have absorbed that unjust and unholy jealousy through which *death came into the world.*[18]

4. For this is what the Scripture says: [19] *And after some days Cain offered to God a sacrifice from the fruits of the earth, and Abel, for his part, offered of the first-born of his flock and of their fat. 2 And God looked kindly on Abel and his gifts, but paid no attention to Cain and his sacrifices. 3 Then Cain was greatly disturbed, and his countenance fell. 4 And God said to Cain: " Why are you disturbed, and why has your countenance fallen? When you offer rightly, but do not rightly discriminate, do you not sin?*[20] *5 Be calm: to you it will return, and you shall dispose of it." 6 And Cain said to his brother Abel: " Let us go out into the field." And this is what happened when they were in the field: Cain set upon his brother Abel and slew him.* 7 You see, brethren, jealousy and envy brought on fratricide. 8 Jealousy was the reason for our father Jacob's flight from his brother Esau.[21] 9 Jealousy caused Joseph to be persecuted with deadly intent and finally to end in servitude. 10 Jealousy compelled Moses to flee from Pharao, king of Egypt, when he heard his fellow tribes-man say: [22] "*Who has appointed you to be ruler and judge over us? Do you mean to kill me as you killed the Egyptian yesterday?*" 11 Through jealousy Aaron and Miriam lodged outside the camp.[23] 12 Jealousy sent Dathan and Abiron alive to Hades, because they had rebelled against Moses, the servant of God. 13 Because of jealousy David not only in-curred the envy of strangers, but was even persecuted by Saul, king of Israel.[24]

5. But, to drop the examples furnished by antiquity. Let us come to the athletes nearest to us in time.[25] Let us take the noble examples of our own generation. 2 It was due to jealousy and envy that the greatest and most holy pillars [26] were persecuted and fought to the death. 3 Let us pass in review the good Apostles: 4 Peter, who through unmerited jealousy underwent not one or two, but many hardships and, after thus giving testimony,[27] departed for the place of glory that was his due. 5 Through jealousy and strife Paul demon-strated how to win the prize of patient endurance: 6 seven times he was imprisoned; he was forced to leave and stoned; [28] he preached in the East and the West; and, finally, he won the splendid renown which his faith had earned. 7 He taught the right manner of life to the whole world, travelled as far as the Western boundary,[29] and, when he had given testi-mony before the authorities, ended his earthly career and was taken up into the holy place as the greatest model of patient endurance.

6. These men who had led holy lives were joined by a great multitude [30] of the elect that suffered numerous indigni-ties and tortures through jealousy and thus became illustrious examples among us.[31] Owing to jealousy, persecuted Danaids and Dircae [32] suffered frightful and abominable outrages and,

securely reaching the goal in the racecourse of the faith, obtained a noble prize, in spite of the weakness of their sex. 3 Jealousy estranged wives from husbands, and thus perverted the saying of our father Adam: [33] *This is now bone of my bones and flesh of my flesh.* 4 Jealousy and strife have laid mighty cities low and uprooted powerful nations.

7. We are writing this, beloved, not merely for your admonition, but also to serve as a reminder to ourselves; for we are in the same arena and face the same conflict. 2 Let us, then, give up those empty and futile aspirations, and turn to the glorious and venerable rule of our tradition. 3 Let us attend to what is noble, what is pleasing, what is acceptable in the sight of our Maker. 4 Let us fix our gaze upon the Blood of Christ and understand how precious it is to the Father,[34] because, poured out for our salvation, it brought to the whole world the grace of conversion. 5 Let us pass in review all the generations and learn the lesson, that from generation to generation the Master *has given an opportunity for conversion*[35] to those who were willing to turn to Him. 6 Noe preached the need of conversion,[36] and such as heeded him were saved. 7 Jonas announced destruction to the Ninevites: [36a] they did penance for their sins and by their prayers propitiated God and gained salvation, although they were not of God's own people.[37]

8. The ministers of the grace of God exhorted through the Holy Spirit to conversion, 2 and the Master of the universe Himself exhorted to conversion with an oath: [38] *As truly as I live, says the Lord, I do not desire the death of the sinner, but his conversion;* and He added a kindly declaration: 3 *House of Israel, be converted from your iniquity. Say to the children of my People: should your sins reach from earth to heaven, and should they be redder than scarlet and blacker*

than sackcloth, and should you turn to me with all your heart and say, "Father!" I will listen to you as a consecrated People. 4 And in another passage He says as follows: [39] *Wash and be cleansed and put away from your souls the wickedness which offends my eyes, rid yourselves of your evil doings, learn to do good, strive for justice, rescue the oppressed, sustain the rights of the orphan, and see justice done to the widow. Then come and let us argue together,*[40] *says the Lord; and should your sins be like purple, I will make them white as snow; and should they be like scarlet, I will make them white as wool; and if you are willing and listen to me, you shall eat the good things of the land; but if you are not willing and do not listen to me, the sword shall devour you. Thus has the mouth of the Lord spoken.* 5 It follows that He wants all His beloved to have a chance to be converted, and this He has ratified by His Almighty Will.

9. Therefore let us comply with His magnificent and glorious purpose, and let us crave His mercy and loving-kindness on bended knee, and turn to His compassion, after abandoning our vain efforts and our strife and the jealousy which but leads to death. 2 Let us fix our gaze upon those who have ministered so perfectly to His transcendent glory. 3 Let us take Enoch [41] who proved irreproachable in obedience and was translated without a trace of his death. 4 Noe [42] proved faithful in discharging his sacred duty and preached a rebirth for the world, and through him the Master saved all those living beings that peacefully entered the Ark.

10. Abraham, called the Friend,[43] proved faithful in being obedient to the words of God. 2 Through obedience this man quit his country, his kith and kin, and his father's house, in order that by turning his back upon a little country, a slender relationship, and a small home, he might inherit the blessings promised by God. For He said to him: " 3 *Quit your country, your kith and kin, and your father's house, and go to the country which I will point out to you; and I will make you the father of a mighty nation, and bless and exalt you, and you shall be blessed; and I will bless those that bless you, and curse those that curse you; and through you all the tribes of the earth shall be blessed.* 4 And again, when he separated from Lot, God said to him: "*Lift your eyes, and from the place where you now are look toward the North and the South and the East and the West; for all the land which you see I will give to you and your posterity to hold forevermore.* 5 *And I will make your posterity as numerous as the dust of the earth: if anyone can number the dust of the earth, then your posterity also can be numbered.* 5 And again it is said: "*God led Abraham out and said to him: " Look up at heaven and count the stars if you can count them: so numerous shall your posterity be!" Abraham believed God, and it was credited to him as justice.* 7 Because of his faith and hospitality, a son was granted him in old age; and through obedience he offered him as a sacrifice to God on one of the mountains He had pointed out to him."

11. Hospitality and piety were the reason for Lot's delivery from Sodom, while the whole surrounding country was chastized by means of fire and brimstone." Thus the Master made it clear that He does not abandon such as hope in Him, but those of a refractory disposition He gives over to chastisement and torture. 2 For example, his wife, who was of a refractory nature and not in complete harmony with him, joined him in going forth, yet she was made a permanent memorial: she was turned into a pillar of salt to this day. It was to be made known to all that the double-minded and those who question the power of God become a warning example of condemnation to all generations.

12. Hospitality and faith were the reason [49] why the harlot Rahab was saved. 2 For when spies had been sent out to Jericho by Jesus, the son of Nave, the king of the land learned that they had come to reconnoiter the territory, and he sent out men to intercept them, so that they might be put under arrest and executed. 3 Now, the hospitable Rahab [50] received the spies in her home and hid them upstairs under flax straw. 4 And when the king's men confronted her and said: *There are men in your house who have come to spy out our country; bring them out, for such is the king's order*, this woman replied: *Yes, the men for whom you are looking did enter my house; but they left at once and are now on their way*; and then she pointed in the opposite direction. 5 And she said to the spies: *I know for a certainty that the Lord God is delivering this land into your hands, for alarm and fear of you have seized its inhabitants. So, when you succeed in conquering it, save me and my father's house.* 6 And they said to her: *Very well; your request shall be granted. As soon, then, as you learn that we are approaching, gather all your people under your roof, and they will be spared; for all that are found outside the house shall perish.* 7 And they further gave her a sign: she was to hang out of her window a scarlet cloth, whereby they made it clear to all that through the Blood of the Lord all those that believe and hope in God would be redeemed. 8 You see, beloved, that the woman possessed not only faith but also the gift of prophecy.

13. Let us, therefore, brethren, be of a humble frame of mind, ridding ourselves of all arrogance and haughtiness and foolishness and passion, and do what the Scripture says; for the Holy Spirit declares: [51] *Let not the wise man boast of his wisdom, or the strong man of his strength, or the rich man of his riches; but, if anyone boasts, let his boast be in the Lord; thus he will seek and do what is right and just.* Especially let us be mindful of the words of the Lord Jesus which He spoke when inculcating gentleness and long-suffering. 2 This is what He said: [52] *Show mercy, that you may be shown mercy; forgive, that you may be forgiven; as you treat others, so you shall be treated; as you give, so you shall receive; as you judge, so you shall be judged; as you show kindness, so kindness shall be shown to you; the measure you use in measuring shall be used in measuring out your share.* 3 With this commandment and these precepts let us strengthen ourselves, that we may live in obedience to His holy words, with humility in our hearts; for the Holy Scripture says: [53] 4 *On whom shall I look but on him who is gentle and meek and trembles at hearing my words?*

14. It is right and holy, therefore, brethren, that we should be submissive to God rather than follow those who through arrogance and insubordination are the ringleaders in a quarrel fomented by detestable jealousy. 2 No ordinary harm, surely, but serious danger shall we incur if we recklessly yield to the caprices of men who plunge into strife and sedition to estrange us from the cause of right. 3 Let us be kind to one another in imitation of the compassion and goodness of our Maker. 4 For the Scripture says: [54] *The kind shall inhabit the land, and the innocent shall be left in possession of it; but the transgressors shall be exterminated.* 5 And again it says: [55] *I saw a godless man rear his head to unseemly heights like the cedars of Lebanon; and I passed by, and behold, he was no more! And I searched for his place,* *and I did not find it. Cherish guilelessness and aim at sincerity, for posterity belongs to the peaceable man.*

15. Therefore let us associate with those who piously cultivate peace, and not with those whose peaceful intentions are but a mask. 2 For somewhere it is said: [56] *This people honors me with its lips; but its heart is far away from me.* 3 And again: *With their lips they blessed, but with their hearts they cursed.* 4 And again it is said: [57] *They loved Him with their lips, and with their tongue they lied to Him; but their heart was not sincere with Him, nor did they prove faithful to His covenant. 5 Therefore struck dumb shall be the treacherous lips that speak evil against the good man.* And again: *May the Lord destroy all the deceitful lips, the boastful tongue, the men that say: " Great glory will we win by our tongue, our lips are our own: who is lord over us? " 6 Because of the wretchedness of the needy and the sighs of the poor, I will now rise, says the Lord; I will bring relief, 7 and boldly will I act in bringing it.*

16. For it is to the humble-minded that Christ belongs, not to those who exalt themselves above His flock. 2 The Sceptre of the Divine Majesty, the Lord Jesus Christ, did not, for all His power, come clothed in boastful pomp and overweening pride, but in a humble frame of mind, as the Holy Spirit has told concerning Him; for He says: [58] 3 *Lord, who has believed our teaching? And the arm of the Lord—to whom has it been revealed? Looking at Him, we announced, as it were, a child, a root, as it were, in thirsty ground; there is no shape, no comeliness in Him; yes, we saw Him, and neither shape nor beauty did He have; but His shape was dishonorable and shrunken beside the shape of men; a man covered with wounds and the marks of hardship; one acquainted with infirmity; because His face is turned away, He* has been dishonored and held in disrespect. 4 Our sins it is that this Man bears, and for our sake He is in pain; and we regarded Him as one afflicted and bruised and ill-treated. 5 But He was wounded for our sins, and languishes because of our iniquities; to give us peace He is under chastisement; by His bruises we were healed. 6 We all, like sheep, had gone astray; each man had wandered from his path. 7 And the Lord delivered Him up for our sins; yet He does not, because He is abused, open His mouth. As a sheep He was led to the slaughter, and as a lamb dumb before the shearer He does not open His mouth. Because of His abasement His condemnation was taken away. 8 As to His generation—who can fathom their minds? From the land of the living is He removed! 9 Because of the iniquities of my people is He come to death! 10 But I will deliver up the wicked for putting Him in the grave, and the rich for putting Him to death; for evil He has not done, nor was guile found on His lips. And the Lord is pleased to free Him from His evil plight. 11 If you make an offering for sin, you will see a long-lived posterity. 12 And the Lord is pleased to take away the torment of His soul, to show Him light, and mold Him through understanding, and thus to render justice to a just man who served many well; and He will take upon Himself the burden of their sins. 13 For this reason He shall count a numerous inheritance and divide the spoils taken from the strong, because He was delivered up to death and classed among the lawless. 14 And He took upon Himself the sins of many, and to atone for their sins He was delivered up. 15 And again He says Himself: [59] I am a worm and not a man, a disgrace among men and the contempt of the people. 16 All that saw me mocked at me; they hissed at me, they shook their heads: " He trusted in the Lord: let the Lord *deliver Him, let Him save Him, for He likes Him."* 17 You see, beloved, what the example is that has been given us; for, if the Lord was so humble-minded, what ought we to do who have come under the influence of His grace through Him?

17. Let us imitate the example of those also who wandered about *dressed in sheepskins and goatskins,* [60] heralding the advent of Christ. We mean the Prophets Elias and Eliseus, as well as Ezechiel; and in addition to these, the men of attested merit. 2 Abraham's merit was magnificently attested,[61] and he was styled a *friend of God*; still, fixing his gaze upon the majesty of God, he said: *But I am dust and ashes.* 3 Furthermore, concerning Job the Scripture says: [62] *Job was good and irreproachable, sincere, God-fearing, who refrained from all evil.* 4 Still, for his part, he accused himself in these words: *No man is clean from defilement, even should his life last but one day.* 5 Moses was called *faithful in all his house,* and God made use of his services to chastize Egypt with the shameful scourges inflicted on them; but even he, though magnificently honored, did not use boastful language; on the contrary, when granted a revelation from the bush, he said: [63] *Who am I that Thou sendest me? I am feeble of speech and slow of tongue.* 6 And again: *I am but steam from a pot.*

18. And what shall we say of David and his attested merit? It was he of whom God said: [64] *I have found a man after my own heart—David, the son of Jesse; in everlasting mercy have I anointed him.* 2 But he, too, says to God: [65] *Have mercy on me, O God, according to Thy great mercy; and according to the multitude of Thy compassions, blot out my iniquity. 3 Wash me more and more from my iniquity, and cleanse me from my sin; for I acknowledge my iniquity, and my sin is ever before my eyes. 4 Against Thee alone have*

I sinned, and what is evil in Thy sight have I done. Thou, therefore, art pronounced just in Thy words, and art acquitted when Thou art tried. 5 For, behold, I was conceived in iniquity, and in sin has my mother been pregnant with me. 6 Behold, Thou lovest sincerity of heart; the hidden secrets of Thy wisdom hast Thou revealed to me. 7 Sprinkle me with hyssop, and I shall be cleansed; wash me, and I shall be whiter than snow. 8 Fill my ears with joy and gladness, and my battered bones shall exult for joy. 9 Turn Thy face away from my sins, and blot out all my iniquities. 10 A pure heart create in me, O God, and renew a right spirit in my inmost soul. 11 Do not reject me from Thy presence, and Thy Holy Spirit do not take away from me. 12 Restore to me the bliss of Thy salvation, and with a princely spirit strengthen me. 13 The wicked will I teach Thy ways, and the impious shall be converted to Thee. 14 Deliver me from bloodguiltiness, O God, my Savior God! 15 My tongue shall exult in Thy justice. Open my mouth, O Lord, and my lips shall proclaim Thy praise. 16 For, hadst Thou wished a sacrifice, I would have offered it; but in whole burnt offerings Thou takest no delight. 17 A sacrifice to God is a contrite spirit; a contrite and humble heart God will not despise.

19. The spirit of humility and modesty, therefore, of so many and thus well-attested men has by their obedience been helpful not only to us, but also to the generations before us, as well as to those who have received His words in fear and truth.[66] 2 And so, since we are allowed to profit by so many glorious examples,[67] let us hasten on to the goal of peace handed down to us from the beginning, and let us fix our gaze upon the Father and Creator of the whole world and hold fast to His magnificent and superabundant gifts and blessings of peace. 3 Let us see Him in spirit, and contemplate with the eyes of the soul His forbearing disposition; let us consider how unimpassioned He is in dealing with all of His creation.[68]

20. The heavens revolve by His arrangement and are subject to Him in peace. 2 Day and night complete the revolution ordained by Him, and neither interferes in the least with the other. 3 Sun and moon and the starry choirs, obedient to His arrangement, roll on in harmony, without any deviation, through their appointed orbits. 4 The earth bears fruit according to His will in its proper seasons, and yields the full amount of food required for men and beasts and all the living things on it, neither wavering nor altering any of His decrees. 5 The unsearchable decisions that govern the abysses and the inscrutable decisions that govern the deeps are maintained by the same decrees. 6 The basin of the boundless sea, firmly built by His creative act for the collecting of the waters, does not burst the barriers set up all around it, and does precisely what has been assigned to it. 7 For He said: [69] *Thus far shalt thou come, and thy billows shall be turned to spray within thee.* 8 The ocean, impassable for men, and the worlds beyond it are governed by the same decrees of the Master.[70] 9 The seasons—spring, summer, autumn, and winter—make room for one another in peaceful succession. 10 The stations of the winds at the proper time render their service without disturbance. Ever-flowing springs, created for enjoyment and for health, without fail offer to men their life-sustaining breasts. The smallest of the animals meet in peaceful harmony. 11 All these creatures the mighty Creator and Master of the universe ordained to act in peace and concord, thus benefitting the universe, but most abundantly ourselves who have taken refuge under His mercies through our Lord Jesus Christ; 12 to whom be the glory and majesty forever and evermore. Amen.[71]

21. Take care, beloved, that His blessings, numerous as they are, do not turn to our condemnation in case we do not—through a life unworthy of Him—do with perfect accord what is good and pleasing in His sight. 2 For somewhere it is said: [72] *The Spirit of the Lord is a lamp that searches the deep recesses of the soul.* 3 Let us understand how nigh He is, and that none of the thoughts we entertain or the plans we devise are hidden from Him. 4 It is right, therefore, that we should not desert the place His will has assigned to us. 5 Rather than to God, let us give offence to silly, unreasoning men, to men conceited and arrogantly indulging in boastful speech. 6 Let us reverence the Lord Jesus Christ, whose Blood was sacrificed for us; respect our officials, honor the presbyters; subject the young to the discipline of the fear of God; train our wives in all that is good. 7 Let these exhibit lovable and chaste manners, show forth a sincere and gentle disposition; by their silence let them manifest their courtesy of speech; without partiality let them perform their works of charity, and with a pure intention bestow them equally on all that fear God. 8 Our children must have their share of a Christian upbringing; they must learn how effective with the Lord is a humble frame of mind, what holy love can accomplish with God, how honorable and excellent is the fear of Him, and how it brings salvation to all who in this fear lead holy lives, with a conscience undefiled. 9 For a searcher is He of thoughts and designs.[73] His breath indwells in us, and when it pleases Him, He can take it away.

22. To all these precepts the faith in Christ gives stability; for He Himself through the Holy Spirit calls us to

31

Him as follows: [74] *Come, children, listen to me: I will teach you the fear of the Lord. 2 Where is the man that desires life, that loves to see good days? 3 Restrain thy tongue from evil speech. and thy lips from speaking guile. 4 Turn away from evil and do what is good. 5 Seek peace and go in pursuit of it. 6 The eyes of the Lord rest upon the good, and His ears attend to their petition. But the frown of the Lord is upon evildoers, to extirpate the memory of them. 7 The good man cried aloud, and the Lord heard him and delivered him from all his afflictions. 8 Many are the plagues of the sinner, but mercy will encompass those that hope in the Lord.*

23. The all-merciful and beneficent Father has compassion on such as fear Him; willingly and with tender regard He bestows His graces on such as approach Him single-minded. 2 Therefore let us not be double-minded, and let not our soul mistrust, seeing His gifts are all-surpassing and glorious. 3 May the Scripture text never apply to us that says: [75] *Wretched are the double-minded, who doubt in their heart and say: " We have heard these things even in the days of our fathers; but, mark you, we have grown old and nothing of all this has happened to us! "* 4 *You fools! Compare yourselves to a tree. Take a vine: first it sheds its foliage; then it puts forth a bud; then a leaf; then a flower; and after that, a green, sour grape; finally, there is a bunch of fresh, ripe grapes.* You see, it takes but a short time to bring the fruit of the plant to maturity. 5 In truth, quickly and suddenly will His will be accomplished, as also the Scripture testifies when it says: [76] *Quickly will He come and will not tarry; and suddenly will the Lord come to His temple—the Holy One, for whom you are looking.*

24. Let us consider, beloved, how the Master continually calls our attention to the future resurrection, the first fruits of which He has made the Lord Jesus Christ by raising Him from the dead."" 2 Let us consider, beloved, the kind of resurrection that occurs at regular intervals. 3 Day and night give us examples of resurrection. The night sleeps, the day rises; the day departs, the night comes on. 4 Let us take the crops. The sowing—how and in what manner does it take place? 5 The sower goes out and puts each of the seeds into the soil: when they fall on the soil, they are dry and bare, and decay. But once they have decayed, the Master's wondrous Providence makes them rise, and each one increases and brings forth multiple fruit."⁸

25. Let us consider the strange and striking phenomenon which takes place in the East, that is, in the regions of Arabia. 2 There is a bird which is called the phoenix.'⁹ It is the only individual of its kind, and it lives five hundred years; and when it approaches dissolution and its death is imminent, it makes itself a nest out of frankincense and myrrh and the other spices; this it enters when the time is fulfilled, and dies. 3 But out of the decaying flesh a sort of worm is born, which feeds on the juices of the dead animal until it grows wings; then, upon growing strong, it takes up that nest in which the bones of the former bird are, and these it carries all the way from Arabia to the Egyptian city called Heliopolis; 4 and there, in daytime, in the sight of all, it lights upon the altar of the Sun and deposits them there, and then departs to its former home. 5 The priests then examine the public records, and find that it has come after the lapse of five hundred years.

26. Do we, then, consider it a great and remarkable thing if the Creator of the universe will bring about a resurrection of those who have piously served Him in the assurance engendered by honest faith, when He uses even a bird to illustrate the sublime nature of His promise? 2 For somewhere it is said: [80] *And Thou wilt raise me, and I will give Thee praise*: and, *I lay down to sleep, and I slept; and I awoke again, for Thou art with me.* 3 And, again, Job says: [81] *Thou wilt raise up this body of mine, which has patiently endured all these things.*

27. Supported, therefore, by this hope, let our souls cling to Him who is faithful in His promises [82] and just in His judgments. 2 He who has enjoined us not to lie will for that reason be Himself all the less capable of lying; for nothing is impossible to God except being untrue to Himself. 3 Let, then, our faith in Him be fanned afresh in us, and let us understand that all things are within His reach. 4 By His majestic command He established the universe, and by a command He can destroy it. 5 *Who shall say to Him: "What hast Thou done?" Or who can resist His mighty strength?* [83] When He wills and as He wills, He can do all things, and nothing once decreed by Him can cease to exist. 6 All things are face to face with Him, and nothing is hidden from His counsel, 7 since *the heavens declare the glory of God, and the firmament proclaims His handiwork; day speaks out to day, and night imparts knowledge to night; and there is not a word, there is not a speech, but its voice is heard.* [84]

28. Since, then, all things are seen and heard, let us stand in awe of Him, and abandon accursed hankerings after evil deeds: thus shall we by His mercy find shelter from the judgment to come. 2 Indeed, whither can anyone of us flee from His mighty hand? What world is there to receive anyone deserting Him? For somewhere the Writing says: [85] 3 *Whither shall I go, and where hide from His face? If I should mount to heaven, Thou art there; if I should depart*

*to the ends of the earth, Thy right hand is there; if I should
lie down in the abyss, Thy Spirit is there.* 4 Whither, then,
can a man depart, or whither run away, from Him who
embraces the universe?

29. Let us, then, approach Him in holiness of soul,
raising pure and unsullied hands to Him, loving our forbearing and compassionate Father, who has made us His chosen
portion. 2 For thus the Scripture says: [86] *When the Most
High was dividing the nations and dispersing the sons of
Adam, He fixed the bounds of the nations according to the
number of God's angels; but Jacob, His People, became the
portion of the Lord, and Israel His apportioned inheritance.*
3 And in another passage it says: [87] *Behold, the Lord made
His own a people from among the nations, just as a man
reserves to himself the first fruits of his threshing floor; and
from that nation shall come forth the Holy of Holies.*

30. Since, then, we are a holy portion, let us do nothing
but what makes for holiness, shunning slander, foul and
sinful embraces, drunkenness and revolutionary desires and
abominable passions, detestable adultery, and abominable
pride. 2 *For God*, it is said,[88] *resists the proud, but gives grace
to the humble.* 3 Let us therefore associate with those on
whom divine grace has been bestowed; let us with humble
minds put on the livery of concord, be self-restrained, keep
ourselves free from all backbiting and slanderous talk; and
let us seek justification by actions, and not just words. 4 For
it is said: [89] *He who speaks much is bound to hear much in
return; or does the idle talker imagine he is always right?
5 Blessed is the woman-born that is short-lived. Do not become a wordy babbler.* 6 Let our praise rest with God,[90] and
not spring from ourselves; for God hates those that praise
themselves. 7 Let the testimony to our good conduct be

given by others, just as it was given to our fathers, those holy men. 8 Rashness, willfulness, and boldness belong to such as are cursed by God; mildness, humility, and gentleness are at home with those blessed by God.

31. Let us, then, cling to His blessing, and study the ways and means of securing this blessing. Let us unroll the records of antiquity.[91] 2 For what reason was our father Abraham blessed? Was it not that he did what was right and lived up to the truth, enabled by faith? 3 With confidence because he knew the future, Isaac cheerfully let himself be led to the altar. 4 Jacob was humble enough to leave his country because of his brother, and went to Laban and lived in servitude; and the twelve tribes were given to him.

32. Whoever considers these details without bias will appreciate the splendor of the gifts conferred by Him. 2 For to him all priests and Levites, the men that served the altar of God, trace their origin; to him, too, the Lord Jesus according to the flesh;[92] to him kings and rulers and princes after Juda; nor are his other tribes in slight esteem, since God had promised:[93] *Thy posterity shall be as numerous as the stars of heaven.* 3 Consequently, all were honored and made great, not through themselves or their own works or the holy lives they led, but through His will. 4 So we, too, who have been called by His will in Christ Jesus, are sanctified not through ourselves, or through our wisdom or understanding or piety or any works we perform in holiness of heart, but through the faith[94] through which Almighty God has sanctified all men from the beginning of time. To Him be the glory forever and evermore. Amen.

33. What, then, are we to do, brethren?[95] Shall we rest from doing good, and give up love? May the Master never permit that this should happen, at least not to us; but let us be eager to perform *every good work* [96] with assiduity and readiness. 2 Why, the Creator and Master of the universe Himself exults in His works. 3 Thus, by His transcendent might He established the heavens, and by His incomprehensible understanding He ordered them: the earth He separated from the water now encircling it, and firmly grounded it on the unshakable foundation of His own will; the creatures which live and move in it He bade come into existence by His own command; to the sea and the beings living in it He assigned, with foresight and by His own power, definite bounds. 4 Finally, the most excellent and greatest being, man, He formed with His sacred and faultless hands in the likeness of His own image. 5 For this is what God says: [97] *Let us create man according to our own image and likeness. And God created man; male and female He created them.* 6 And then, when He had finished all these things, He praised and blessed them, and said: [98] *Increase and multiply.* 7 Let us realize that everywhere holy men feel honored by their good works, and that the Lord Himself rejoiced at having honored Himself by good works. 8 With this pattern before us, let us unhesitatingly submit to His will: with all our strength let us achieve the work of sanctification.

34.   The good workman with assurance receives the bread of his labor; the slack and slothful cannot look his employer full in the face. 2 It is our duty, therefore, to be prompt to do good; for on Him depends everything. 3 Indeed, He says to us by way of warning: [99] *Here comes the Lord, and with Him comes the award He makes, to pay each one according to His work.* 4 He urges us on, therefore, to trust in Him with all our heart and not to be slack and indolent in *any good work.* [100] 5 Let Him be our boast and the ground of our confidence; let us be subject to His will; let us consider the vast multitude of His angels, and see how they stand in readiness to minister to His will. 6 For the Scripture says:[101] *Ten thousand times ten thousand stood ready before Him, and thousand times one thousand ministered to Him, and cried out: " Holy, Holy, Holy is the Lord of hosts; the whole creation is replete with His splendor."* 7 And so we, too, being dutifully assembled with one accord,[102] should, as with one voice, cry out to Him earnestly, so that we may participate in His great and glorious promises. 8 For it is said:[103] *Eye has not seen, and ear has not heard, and heart of man has not conceived, what He has prepared for those that await Him patiently.*

35. How blessed, beloved, and marvellous are the gifts of God! 2 Life with immortality; joyousness with observance of the law; truth with boldness; faith with confidence; continence with holiness! And all these blessings even now fall within our comprehension! 3 What, then, are the things that are prepared for those who wait patiently! The Creator and Father of the ages, the All-holy, alone grasps their number and beauty. 4 Let us, therefore, exert ourselves to be found in the number of those who patiently wait for Him, so that we may participate in the promised gifts. 5 But how, beloved, can this be done? If our mind is faithfully fixed on God; if we seek out what is pleasing and acceptable to Him; if we carry out what His irreprehensible will demands, and follow the way of truth, by ridding ourselves of *every vice and wickedness, of avarice, strife, malice and fraud, gossip and slander, hatred of God, pride and arrogance,* conceit and inhospitality. 6 For those who practice these things are hateful to God; *and not only those that do such things, but also those that countenance them.*[104] 7 For the Scripture says:[105]

*But to the sinner God said: "Why do you speak of my
ordinances and why do you have my covenant on your lips?
8 You hated discipline and paid no attention to my words.
Whenever you saw a thief, you ran along with him; and
with adulterers you threw in your lot. Your mouth brimmed
over with malice, and your tongue wove treacherous plots.
There you sat backbiting and laying a snare for your very
brother. 9 This you did, and I kept silent. You, man without
principles, supposed that I should be like you! 10 I will put
you in the wrong, and show you to yourself in your true light!
11 Now, take my words to heart, you who are forgetting God;
or else He will like a lion carry you off, with no one to rescue
you. 12 A sacrifice of praise will honor me, and there is the
way in which I will show him the salvation of man."*

36. This, beloved, is the way in which we found our
salvation, Jesus Christ, the High Priest[106] who offers our
gifts, the patron and helper in our weakness. 2 It is through
Him that we look straight at the heavens above. Through
Him we see mirrored God's faultless and transcendent countenance.[107] Through Him the eyes of our heart were opened.
Through Him our unintelligent and darkened mind shoots
up into the light. Through Him the Master was pleased to
let us taste the knowledge that never fades; for,[108] *being Himself the radiance of His splendor, He towers as much above
the angels as the title He has inherited is superior to theirs.*
3 For thus the Scripture says:[109] *He appointed winds to be
His angels, and fiery flames His ministers.* 4 But about His
Son the Master spoke thus: *Thou art my Son: this day have
I begotten Thee. Ask of me, and I will give Thee the nations
for Thy inheritance, and the vast, wide earth for Thy possession.* 5 And again He says to Him:[110] *Be seated at my right
hand, until I make Thy foes a footstool for Thy feet.*

6 Now, who are the foes? The wicked and those who run counter to His will.

37. Let us, then, brethren, do soldier's duty in downright earnest under the banner of His glorious commands. 2 Let us observe those who are soldiering under our commanders, and see how punctually, how willingly, how submissively they execute the commands! 3 Not all are prefects, or tribunes, or centurions, or lieutenants, and so on; but *each in his own rank* [111] executes the orders of the emperor and the commanders. 4 The great cannot exist without the small, nor can the small without the great. A certain organic unity binds all parts, and therein lies the advantage. 5 Let us take our body. [112] The head is nothing without the feet, and the feet are nothing without the head. *The smallest organs* of our body are necessary and valuable to the whole body; in fact, all parts conspire and yield the same obedience toward maintaining the whole of the body.

38. Therefore let the whole of our body [113] be maintained in Christ Jesus, and let each submit to his neighbor's rights in the measure determined by the special gift bestowed on him. [114] 2 Let the strong care for the weak, and the weak respect the strong; let the rich support the poor, and the poor render thanks to God for giving them the means of supplying their needs; [115] let the wise man show his wisdom not in words but in active help; the humble man must not testify for himself, but leave it to another to testify in his behalf. He who is continent [116] must not boast, knowing that it is another who confers on him the ability to remain continent. 3 Let us therefore reflect, brethren, of what clay we were made, what and who we were when we entered the world, out of what grave and darkness our Maker and Creator has brought us into the world, where He had prepared His benefits before our birth. 4 Since, then, we owe all these blessings to Him, we are obliged to thank Him in every way. To Him be the glory forever and evermore. Amen.

39. Witless, unintelligent, foolish, and uninstructed persons mock and sneer at us because they have an overweening opinion of themselves. 2 Really—what can a mortal do? Or, what strength is there in an earth-born creature? 3 For the Scripture says: [117] *There was no shape before my eyes; but only a breath and sound I heard. 4 How could it be otherwise? Can a mortal be pure in the sight of the Lord, or a man blameless in his actions, when He does not trust His servants and has noted some perversity in His angels? 5 Heaven is not pure in His sight—and we should be!—we who are dwelling in houses of clay, the same clay of which we ourselves are made! They are crushed as one crushes a moth, and they last not from morn to eventide. Unable to help themselves, they perished. 6 He breathed on them, and they died because of their lack of wisdom. 7 Raise your voice in appeal, and see if anyone will answer you, if one of His holy angels you will behold! For haughtiness destroys the witless man, and passion slays the wayward one. 8 I have seen it—uprooted is the fool, and his abode is suddenly consumed. 9 Beyond the reach of help his children are and insulted at the gates of lesser men, and there is no one to deliver them. What they have hoarded up the good shall eat, while they themselves shall not be rescued from calamity.*

40. Since, therefore, this is evident to all of us, and we have explored the depths of the divine knowledge, [118] we are obliged to carry out in fullest detail what the Master has commanded us to do at stated times. 2 He has ordered the sacrifices to be offered and the services to be held, and this not in a random and irregular fashion, but at definite times and seasons. 3 He has, moreover, Himself, by His sovereign will determined where and by whom He wants them to be carried out. Thus all things are done religiously, acceptable to His good pleasure, dependent on His will. 4 Those, therefore, that make their offerings at the prescribed times are acceptable and blessed; for, since they comply with the ordinances of the Master, they do not sin.[119] 5 Special functions are assigned to the high priest; a special office is imposed upon the priests; and special ministrations fall to the Levites. The layman [120] is bound by the rules laid down for the laity.

41. *Each* of us, brethren, must *in his own place* [121] endeavor to please God with a good conscience, reverently taking care not to deviate from the established rule of service. 2 Not everywhere, brethren, are sacrifices offered—be they perpetual offerings, or votive offerings, or sin offerings, or trespass offerings—but at Jerusalem only; and there offerings are not made in every place, but in front of the sanctuary,[122] where the gift to be offered is inspected for blemishes by the high priest and the aforesaid ministers. 3 Those, therefore, that do anything contrary to what conforms to His will suffer death as the penalty. 4 You see, brethren, that the greater the knowledge vouchsafed to us, the greater the risk we incur.

42. The Apostles preached to us the Gospel received from Jesus Christ, and Jesus Christ was God's Ambassador. 2 Christ, in other words, comes with a message from [123] God, and the Apostles with a message from Christ. Both these orderly arrangements, therefore, originate from the will of God. 3 And so, after receiving their instructions and being fully assured through the Resurrection of our Lord Jesus Christ, as well as confirmed in faith by the word of God, they went forth, equipped with the fullness of the Holy Spirit, to preach the good news that the Kingdom of God was close at hand. 4 From land to land, accordingly, and from city to city [124] they preached, and from among their earliest converts appointed men whom they had tested by the Spirit to act as bishops and deacons for the future believers. 5 And this was no innovation, for, a long time before the Scripture had spoken about bishops and deacons; for somewhere it says: [125] *I will establish their overseers in observance of the law and their ministers in fidelity.*

43. What wonder, pray, if those entrusted by God through Christ with such an office have appointed the above-mentioned officials, seeing that also the blessed Moses, *the faithful servant in all the house,* [126] has recorded in the sacred books all the injunctions given him; and the other Prophets followed his example and joined him in bearing testimony to the laws given by him. 2 For, when [127] the priesthood had become an object of jealousy and the tribes were quarrelling as to which of them had been honored with that glorious dignity, he ordered the leaders of the twelve tribes to bring him each a rod with the name of his tribe written upon it; and he took the rods and bound them together and sealed them with the rings of the tribe leaders, and then deposited them on the table of God in the Tabernacle of Testimony. 3 He then shut the Tabernacle and sealed the keys just as he had done the rods, 4 and said to them: " Brethren, God has chosen for His priestly service that tribe the rod of which will bud." 5 When day broke, he called a meeting of all Israel, six hundred thousand men in all, showed the seals to the leaders of the tribes, opened the Tabernacle and produced the rods, and it was found that the rod of Aaron had not only put forth buds but also borne fruit. 6 What do you think, brethren? Did not Moses know the outcome beforehand? He certainly did know it; but he acted in this manner to prevent any insubordination in Israel, so that the name of the true and only God [128] might be glorified. To Him be the glory forever and evermore. Amen.

44. Our Apostles, too, were given to understand by our Lord Jesus Christ that the office of the bishop [129] would give rise to intrigues. 2 For this reason, equipped as they were with perfect foreknowledge, they appointed the men mentioned before, and afterwards laid down a rule once for all to this effect: when these men die, other approved men shall succeed to their sacred ministry. 3 Consequently, we deem it an injustice to eject from the sacred ministry the persons who were appointed either by them, or later, with the consent of the whole Church, by other men in high repute and have ministered to the flock of Christ faultlessly, humbly, quietly and unselfishly, and have moreover, over a long period of time, earned the esteem of all. 4 Indeed, it will be no small sin for us if we oust men who have irreproachably and piously offered the sacrifices proper to the episcopate. 5 Happy the presbyters who have before now completed life's journey and taken their departure in mature age and laden with fruit! They, surely, do not have to fear that anyone will dislodge them from the place built for them. [130] 6 Yes, we see that you removed some, their good conduct notwithstanding, from the sacred ministry on which their faultless discharge had shed lustre.

45. You are given to wrangling, brethren, and are jealous in matters that bear upon salvation. [131] 2 You have looked

deep into the sacred writings, which tell the truth and pro-
ceed from the Holy Spirit. 3 You know that nothing unjust
or fraudulent is written in them. [132] You will not find that
law-respecting men were ever repudiated by holy men.
4 Law-respecting men were persecuted of course, but only
by lawless men. They were put in prison, but only by unholy
men. They were stoned to death by contemners of the law.
They were killed by men animated by unjust and abominable
jealousy. 5 Under such ill-treatment they bore up gloriously.
6 What shall we say, brethren? Was Daniel thrown into the
lion's den by God-fearing men? [133] 7 Or, were Ananias,
Azarias, and Misael shut up in the fiery furnace by men
devoted to the glorious and exalted worship of the Most
High? Let no such thing be said! Who, then, were those
that committed such acts? Hateful men and the scum of the
earth carried their love of strife to such a degree of fury that
they subjected to indignities men who were serving God with
holy and irreproachable steadfastness; they did not realize
that the Most High is the champion and shield of those who
in perfect good faith worship His most holy name. To Him
be the glory forever and evermore. Amen. 8 But those who
confidently persevered, inherited honor and glory: they were
exalted and had their names engraved by God in His memory
forever and evermore. Amen.

46. It is our duty, then, my brethren, to follow examples
such as these. 2 For the Scripture says: [134] *Follow the saints,
for such as follow them shall be sanctified.* 3 And again, in
another passage, it says: *With an innocent man Thou wilt
be innocent, and with an elect Thou wilt be elect, and with
one perverted Thou wilt deal perversely.* 4 Let us, therefore,
associate with the innocent and law-abiding; these are God's
elect. 5 Why are quarrels and outbursts of passion and divi-

sions and schisms and war in your midst?[135] 6 Or, do we not
have one God and one Christ and one Spirit of grace, a Spirit
that was poured out upon us? And is there not one calling
in Christ?[136] 7 Why do we tear apart and disjoint the
members of Christ and revolt against our own body, and go to
such extremes of madness as to forget that we are mutually
dependent members?[137] Remember the words of Jesus our
Lord. 8 For He said:[138] *Utterly wretched is that man; it
would be better for him not to have been born than to be an
occasion of sin to one of my elect; it would be better for him
to lie at the bottom of the sea with a millstone hung round his
neck than to pervert one of my elect.* 9 Your schism has perverted many; many it has thrown into discouragement, many
it has bewildered, and to all of us it has brought sorrow.
And your schism persists!

47. Take up the epistle of the blessed Apostle Paul.
2 What is the most important thing he wrote to you *in the
early days of gospel preaching?*[139] 3 He was truly inspired
when he wrote to you regarding *himself and Cephas and
Apollos,*[140] because already at that time you had engaged in
factious agitation. 4 But that display of factiousness involved
you in less guilt, for you took the part of Apostles, men of
attested merit, and of a man in good repute with them. 5 But
now consider who those are that have perverted you and
vilified the venerable character of your celebrated fraternal
charity. 6 Disgraceful, beloved, indeed, exceedingly disgraceful and unworthy of your training in Christ,[141] is the report
that the well-established and ancient Church of the Corinthians is, thanks to one or two individuals, in revolt against
the presbyters. 7 And this report has reached not only us,
but also people that differ from us in religion,[142] with the

result that, owing to your folly, you heap blasphemy upon the name of the Lord and withal create a danger to yourselves.

48. Let us, then, quickly blot out this blemish and fall on our knees before the Master, and with tears implore Him to have mercy on us and be reconciled to us and restore us to the venerable and holy practice of brotherly love. 2 For this is the gate of observance of the law,[143] which opens out into life, as the Scripture says: *Open to me the gates of observance of the law: I will go in by them and praise the Lord.* 3 *This is the gate of the Lord: observers of the law will go in by it.* 4 Of the many open gates, therefore, this gate of observance of the law is the gate of Christ: blessed are all those who enter by it and walk the straight path *in holiness and observance of the law*, performing without disturbance all their duties.[144] 5 Let a man be *a man of faith*,[145] let him be able to utter knowledge, let him be skilled in the discernment of discourses, let him be pure in his conduct; 6 surely, he must think all the less of himself, the higher he apparently ranks, and seek the common good and not his personal advantage.

49. He who has love in Christ must observe the commandments of Christ.[146] 2 The binding power of the love of God[147]—who is able to set it forth? 3 The radiance of His beauty—who can voice it to satisfaction? 4 The sublimity to which love leads up is unutterable. 5 Love unites us with God; *love covers a multitude of sins*;[148] love endures everything, is long-suffering to the last; there is nothing vulgar, nothing conceited, in love; love creates no schism; love does not quarrel; love preserves perfect harmony. In love all the elect of God reached perfection, apart from love nothing is pleasing to God. 6 In love the Master took us to Himself. Because of the love which He felt for us, Jesus Christ Our

4¹

Lord gave His Blood for us by the will of God, His body for our bodies, and His soul for our souls.

50. You see, beloved, how great and wonderful love is, and there is no setting forth its perfection. 2 Who is able to possess it, except those to whom God grants this privilege? Let us, therefore, earnestly beg of His mercy, that we may be found to possess a love unmixed with human partiality and above reproach. 3 All the generations from Adam down to this day have passed away; but those who are perfected in love in the measure of God's grace, have a place among the saints, and they will be made manifest when the Kingdom of Christ comes to visit us. 4 For the Scripture says: [149] *Enter the chambers for a little while, until my anger and fury pass away; then will I remember the good day, and will raise you from your graves.* 5 Happy are we, beloved, if we observe the commandments of the Lord in the concord of love; for thus our sins will be forgiven us through love. 6 For the Scripture says: [150] *Happy those whose iniquities have been forgiven, and whose sins have been covered up; happy the man to whom the Lord will not impute his sin, and on whose lips there is no guile.* 7 This blessing was pronounced on those chosen by God through Jesus Christ our Lord, to whom be the glory forever and evermore. Amen.

51. Let us, then, ask pardon for our waywardness and for what we have done yielding to any wiles of the adversary; but those, too, who were the ringleaders in this quarrel and sedition, ought, for their part, to ponder on the common nature of our hope. 2 Surely, those who live in fear and love prefer that they themselves should suffer indignities rather than their neighbors; they prefer to have reproach cast on themselves rather than on that traditional concord so well and justly established among us. 3 It is better for a man to make a clean breast of his failings than to harden his heart in imitation of those who, after rebelling against God's servant Moses, [151] hardened their hearts, and whose condemnation was brought to light: 4 *alive they went down to Hades, where death shall be their shepherd.* 5 Pharao and his army and all the leaders of Egypt, including the chariots and their riders, were swallowed up by the Red Sea and perished for no other reason than that their foolish hearts were hardened after striking exhibitions of power had been performed in Egypt by God's servant Moses.[152]

52. In need of nothing, brethren, stands the Master of the universe; nothing does He ask of anyone, except that confession should be offered Him; 2 for David the chosen says: [153] *I will confess to the Lord, and it will please Him better than a calf with budding horns and hoofs. Let the poor see it and rejoice.* 3 And again he says: [154] *Sacrifice to God a sacrifice of praise, and pay to the Most High your vows; call upon me in the day of your affliction, and I will rescue you, and you will glorify me.* 4 *For a sacrifice to God is a crushed spirit.*

53. Surely, you are acquainted, beloved, and well acquainted, with the Sacred Scriptures, and have explored the oracles of God; and therefore we write these things merely to serve as a reminder. 2 Now, when Moses [155] had gone up the mountain and spent forty days and forty nights in fasting and chastizing himself, God said to him: *Descend in haste, for your people whom you led out of the land of Egypt, have broken the law; they have quickly deviated from the way you had marked out for them: they have made themselves molten images.* 3 And the Lord said to him: *Once and even*

*twice have I spoken to you thus: I have looked at this people,
and behold, it is stiff-necked; suffer me to exterminate them,
and I will wipe out their name from under heaven; and I
will make you the ruler of a nation mighty and wonderful
and much greater than this one.* 4 Then Moses said: *No, no,
Lord! Forgive this people their sin, or else blot me also out
of the book of the living.* 5 O great charity! O unsurpassed
perfection! A servant speaks boldly to the Lord; he asks
forgiveness for the people, or else that he himself may be
blotted out with them!

54. Now, then, who among you is noble, who compassionate, who full of charity? 2 Let him say: " If I am the
cause of sedition and strife and schism, then I depart; I go
wherever you wish; I do whatever the majority enjoins: only
let the flock of Christ have peace with the appointed presbyters." [156] 3 He who acts thus will win great glory for
himself in Christ, and every place will welcome him; for *the
earth and all that is in it are the Lord's.* [157] 4 Those who live
as citizens of God's Kingdom—a life that never brings regrets
—have acted thus and will act thus.

55. But let us also adduce examples from the heathens.
Many kings and rulers have during a time of pestilence
accepted the advice of oracles and given themselves up to
death in order to rescue by their own blood their fellow
citizens. Many left their own cities to prevent the spread
of a schism. 2 We know of many in our own midst [158] who
gave themselves up to imprisonment in order to ransom
others. Many gave themselves up to slavery, and with the
price they received for themselves, furnished food for others.
3 Many women, invested with power through the grace of
God, have accomplished many a manly deed. 4 The blessed

Judith,[159] when the city was under siege, asked of the elders leave for herself to go out into the camp of the heathens. 5 Exposing herself to danger, therefore, she went out for love of her country and of her people that were in a state of siege, and the Lord delivered Holofernes into the hands of a woman. 6 Nor did Esther,[160] that woman of perfect faith, expose herself to less danger in order to rescue the twelve tribes of Israel from imminent destruction; for by fasting and chastizing her body she implored the all-seeing Master, the God of the ages, and He, seeing her self-abasement, rescued the people for whose sake she had incurred danger.

56. Let us, too, therefore, pray for those who are guilty of some fault, that meekness and humility may be granted them, and incline them to submit—not to us—but to the will of God; thus our compassionate remembrance of them before God and the saints will bear perfect fruit for them. 2 Let us, beloved, accept correction, which no one must take in bad part. A reproof which we administer to one another is honorable and extremely helpful, for it unites us to the will of God. 3 For Holy Writ says as follows:[161] *Severely has the Lord chastized me, but He did not give me over to death. 4 For, him whom the Lord loves He chastizes, and He always scourges the son whom He takes to His heart. 5 For, the good man, it says, will chastize me with mercy and reprove me; but let not the oil of sinners anoint my head. 6 And again it says: Well for the man whom the Lord reproves; and do not reject the correction of the Almighty; for He causes pain, but then He sets things right again; 7 He wounds, but His hands heal again; 8 six times He will extricate you from distress, and the seventh time evil shall not touch you; 9 in famine He will rescue you from death, and in war He will* *deliver you from the grip of the sword; 10 and from the scourge of the tongue will He hide you, and you shall not fear when evils approach; 11 you will laugh at the wicked and lawless, and of wild beasts you shall not be afraid; 12 for wild beasts shall leave you in peace. 13 Then you will find that your house will be undisturbed, and the tent in which you dwell shall not fail; 14 you will find that your posterity will be numerous, and your children will be like the herbs of the field; 15 you will go down into the grave like ripened corn to be harvested at the right time, or like a heap on the threshing-floor that is garnered at the appointed time.* 16 You see, beloved, what great protection awaits those who let themselves be disciplined by the Master; for, being a kind Father, He disciplines us in order that we may obtain mercy through His holy discipline.

57. You, therefore, the prime movers of the schism, submit to the presbyters,[162] and, bending the knees of your hearts, accept correction and change your minds. 2 Learn submissiveness, and rid yourselves of your boastful and proud incorrigibility of tongue. Surely, it is better for you to be little and honorable within the flock of Christ than to be esteemed above your deserts and forfeit the hope which He holds out. 3 For thus the excellent Wisdom says:[163] *Behold, I will speak out the words of my spirit; I will teach you my message. 4 Since I called you and you did not listen, and since I put forth my message and you paid no attention, but set my counsels at naught and disobeyed my warnings: therefore will I in turn laugh at your destruction; and I will exult when ruin overtakes you, and when you are seized suddenly by dismay, and the catastrophe is at hand like a squall, or when distress and siege come upon you. 5 Yes, when you call upon me for help, I will not listen to you. Seek me the* *wicked will, but they will not find me. For they hated wisdom and did not choose the fear of the Lord, and they refused to attend to my counsels and sneered at my reproofs. 6 Therefore they shall eat the fruits of their own way, and be glutted with their own impiousness. 7 Because they wronged the little ones, they shall be slaughtered; and a searching inquiry shall destroy the impious. But he who listens to me will find shelter in hope and confidence and will rest secure from every ill.*

58. Let us, then, be subject to His most holy and glorious name, and escape the threats which Wisdom has uttered in advance against the disobedient. Thus we shall find shelter, firmly reposing on the most holy name of His majesty. 2 Accept our counsel, and you shall have nothing to regret. For, as truly as God lives, as truly as the Lord Jesus Christ and the Holy Spirit live, and the faith and the hope of the elect, so truly will he who in a humble frame of mind, with eagerness to yield, and unregretfully carries out the commandments and precepts given by God, be enrolled and be in good standing among the number of those who are on the way to salvation through Jesus Christ, through whom is to Him the glory forever and evermore. Amen.

59. But should any disobey what has been said by Him through us,[164] let them understand that they will entangle themselves in transgression and no small danger. 2 But for our part we shall be innocent of this sin, and will offer earnest prayer and supplication that the Creator of the universe may preserve undiminished the established number [165] of His elect in all the world through His beloved Son Jesus Christ, through whom He has called us *out of darkness into light,* out of ignorance into the full knowledge of the splendor of

His name, 3 that we may hope in Thy name [166] which gave existence to all creation. Open *the eyes of our heart,*[167] that we may know Thee who alone art *Highest among the highest and Holy, reposing among the holy; who humblest the pride of the haughty, destroyest the designs of the heathens; who raisest up the lowly and humblest the lofty, makest rich and makest poor, slayest and bringest to life;* who alone art the Benefactor *of spirits and the God of all flesh. Thou gazest upon the deep,* Thou beholdest the works of men, the Helper in danger, *the Savior in despair,*[168] the Creator and Watcher of every spirit. Thou multipliest the nations upon the earth, and from among all Thou hast chosen those that love Thee through Jesus Christ, Thy beloved Son, through whom Thou hast instructed, sanctified, and honored us. 4 We beg Thee, O Master, to be our *Helper and Protector:* [169] deliver those of us who are in distress, raise up the fallen, show Thy face to those in need, heal the infirm, bring back the erring of Thy people, feed the hungry, ransom our prisoners, set the infirm upon their feet, comfort the fainthearted: *let all the nations know that Thou art the only God,*[170] that Jesus Christ is Thy Son, *that we are Thy people and the sheep of Thy pasture.*

60. For Thou hast made known the everlasting constitution of the world through *the forces at work in it.*[171] Thou, O Lord, hast created the world, Thou who art faithful in all generations, right in Thy judgments, wonderful in strength and transcendent greatness, wise in creating, and judicious in establishing what has come into being, beneficent throughout the visible world and kind toward those that trust in Thee. *O merciful and compassionate one,*[172] forgive us our iniquities and misdemeanors and transgressions and shortcomings! 2 Do not consider every sin of Thy servants and servant maids; but cleanse us as only Thy truth can cleanse, and *direct our steps to walk in holiness of heart and to do the things which are good and pleasing in Thy sight* and in the sight of our rulers. 3 Yes, Master, *let Thy face beam upon us*,[173] that we may do good in peace and be sheltered *under Thy mighty hand* and delivered from every sin *by Thy uplifted arm*, and deliver us from such as hate us without cause.[174] 4 Grant concord and peace to us as well as to all the inhabitants of the earth, just as Thou didst grant it to our fathers when they piously *called upon Thee in faith and truth;*[175] grant us to be obedient to Thy almighty and glorious name, as well as to our princes and rulers on earth.

61. Thou, O Master, through Thy transcendent and indescribable sovereignty hast given them the power of royalty, so that we, acknowledging the honor and glory conferred upon them by Thee, may bow to them, without in the least opposing Thy will. Grant to them, O Lord, health, peace, concord, and firmness, so that they may without hindrance exercise the supreme leadership Thou hast conferred on them. 2 For it is Thou, O Master, O heavenly *King of all ages*,[176] that conferrest upon the sons of men glory and honor and authority over the things which are upon the earth. Do Thou, O Lord, direct their counsels in accord with what is *good and pleasing in Thy sight*,[177] so that they may piously exercise in peace and gentleness the authority Thou hast granted them, and thus experience Thy graciousness. 3 To Thee, who alone art able to bestow these and even greater blessings upon us, we render thanks and praise through the High Priest and Ruler of our souls, Jesus Christ, through whom be to Thee the glory and majesty now and for all generations and forever and evermore. Amen.[178]

62. What we have written to you, brethren, sufficiently explains what concerns our worship and is most helpful for a virtuous life to those who wish to live piously and dutifully. 2 For, concerning faith and repentance and genuine charity and self-control and sobriety and patient endurance—we have touched upon every subject, and reminded you that you are in duty bound to please Almighty God through piety and truth and long-suffering: you are to live in concord, without bearing malice, in love and peace, joined to constant forbearance. In this manner our forbears, mentioned above, were acceptable and cherished a humble frame of mind toward the Father and God and Creator and all mankind. 3 And we have all the more pleasure in recalling this to your memory because we are well aware that we are writing to persons who are *believers* and highly distinguished and deeply versed in the writings [179] that contain God's educative revelation.

63. It is right, therefore, that we should adhere to so many and such notable examples and bow the neck [180] and discharge the duty of obedience, so that, ceasing from that futile dissension, we may without any blame reach the goal set before us in truth. 2 You certainly will give us the keenest pleasure if you prove obedient to what we have written through the Holy Spirit, and extirpate the lawless passion of your jealousy in accordance with the pleas we have made in this letter for peace and concord. 3 We are sending trustworthy and prudent men, who have led blameless lives among us from youth to old age, that they may be witnesses [181] between you and us. 4 We do this to make you feel that our whole care has been, and is, directed toward establishing speedy peace in your midst.

64. And now may the all-seeing God and Master *of spirits* and Lord *of all flesh*,[182] who chose the Lord Jesus Christ and us through Him to be *a people set apart for Himself*, grant to every soul that invokes His transcendent and holy name—faith, fear, peace, patient endurance and long-suffering, self-control, holiness, and sobriety, so that they may be well-pleasing[183] to His Majesty through our High Priest and Ruler, Jesus Christ, through whom be to Him glory and greatness, power and honor, both now and forever and evermore. Amen.

65. As for our representatives Claudius Ephebus and Valerius Bito, accompanied by Fortunatus, send them back to us at an early convenience, full of peace and joy, that they may without delay bring tidings of peace and concord—the object of our most ardent desires—and that we in turn may without delay rejoice in your tranquillity.

2 May the grace of our Lord Jesus Christ be with you and with all that have anywhere in the world been called by God and through Him, through whom be to Him glory and honor and power and majesty and everlasting dominion, from eternity to eternity. Amen.

CLEMENT'S FIRST EPISTLE TO THE CORINTHIANS[184]

ST. IGNATIUS OF ANTIOCH

EPISTLES

INTRODUCTION

It is a refreshing experience for any religious-minded person of today to shut his eyes for once to the many complex, and in some degree unpleasant, aspects of religious life and look into the soul of a great man who succeeded in reducing this complexity to one or two engrossing facts or ideas and putting them in the centre of his everyday life. One such man was St. Ignatius, bishop of Antioch in Syria at the beginning of the second century, and one such soul was that which he mirrored in his epistles addressed to several Christian communities in Asia Minor. " God " and " Jesus Christ " were the absorbing interests that dominated the world of Ignatius. Here we find a unified *Weltanschauung*, one pivoted on " God " and " Jesus Christ." Here we see portrayed an otherworldliness that was carried to its utmost consequences. And, since in addition to this objective fact we are made aware by the reading of these epistles that their author exhibits charming traits of character, it is small wonder that his epistles are the most beautiful pearls of our extant early Christian literature.[1]

Our information regarding the life of Ignatius is extremely meagre. Besides what the letters themselves reveal of the man, we have only scanty notices preserved by contemporary and some later writers, such as St. Polycarp, St. Irenaeus, Origen, Eusebius, and St. Jerome. Ignatius refers to himself as " also called Theophorus "—that is, " God-bearer "—presumably to indicate that, in the words of St. Paul, his only

" boast " was " God " and " Jesus Christ."² There is a pretty
legend to the effect that he was the little Jewish child whom,
on a certain painful occasion (Matt. 18. 1), Christ singled
out to serve His Apostles as a model of childlike simplicity.
Others have inferred from his name that he was a native of
Syria and a pagan who in his later years embraced Christianity. He is also believed to have been an auditor of the
Apostle St. John.³ It is certain that he was the third bishop
of Antioch, being the second successor to St. Peter. After the
dispersion of the Apostles from Jerusalem, it was in the capital of Syria that the Church's missionary activity among the
pagans was given a vigorous impetus. Here St. Barnabas,
St. Paul, and St. Peter exercised their apostolic zeal; here,
doubtless, surrounded by the edifying lives of many early
converts, Ignatius imbibed his ardent love for Christ; here he
witnessed admirable examples of a faith that made him
immune against the voluptuousness of the Syrian metropolis.
The fact of his martyrdom in the great Flavian Amphitheatre
at Rome, known as the Colosseum, is well attested. This took
place about the year 110 during the reign of the emperor
Trajan. Since the seven epistles were written as he was
being taken under guard from Antioch to Rome, they are
to be cherished as the last utterances of " a condemned man,"
as he himself says, or, as we should say, of a holy man who
could see no more fitting climax to his discipleship than " to
be crunched by the teeth of wild beasts " for Christ's sake.
The Western Church keeps the feast of this athlete of Christ
on February 1, the Eastern, on December 20.

There is no space in this sketch for all the details of the
literary controversy upon the genuineness of the Ignatian
epistles. They have come down to us in a longer and a shorter
form; besides, in the Middle Ages there were no less than

seventeen letters which claimed Ignatian authorship. Unfortunately, the literary problems became involved in the
theological controversies that were waged especially in England, in the seventeenth century, and the dispute was carried
on with heat and bitterness. The great stumbling block in
the way of a more peaceful settlement was the outspoken
insistence of Ignatius on the strictly hierarchical constitution
of the Church. He continually speaks of " bishops, presbyters, and deacons " as men to whom obedience was due,
and of the laity who were bound to obey. The long line of
scholars who engaged in this controversy extends from
Scultetus, Ussher, Dallaeus, and Pearson down to Zahn,
Lightfoot, Harnack, Funk, and many others.[4] At present
competent scholarship on both the Catholic and the Protes-
tant side accepts the seven epistles, on which this translation
is based, as genuinely Ignatian.

The letters of Ignatius are addressed to six Christian communities: the Ephesians, the Magnesians, the Trallians, the
Romans, the Philadelphians, the Smyrnaeans, and to St.
Polycarp, bishop of Smyrna. Ephesus, known to us particularly from the *Acts* and the epistles of St. Paul, was the
capital of the Roman province of Asia.[5] From here, it is
conjectured, St. Paul made missionary excursions to the
neighboring cities of Magnesia by the Maeander, Tralles,
and Philadelphia. The first four of these letters were penned
or dictated by Ignatius during his stay at Smyrna, where his
Roman guards allowed him a brief respite on his toilsome
journey. Here delegates from several cities met Ignatius to
pay him their respects and to offer him such comforts as the
trying circumstances of his captivity permitted. Ignatius
made use of his leisure to write the first three of his letters
to thank his friends for their sympathy, to strengthen them in

their faith, and, above all, to warn them against dangers from
certain heresies that must have been rampant at that time in
that part of Asia Minor. A fourth letter, written to the
Church of the Romans, is markedly different in tone. Here
his chief concern is to beg his Roman friends, some of whom
were doubtless prominent Christians, not to interfere with his
heart's desire by obtaining a stay of the Roman governor's
mandate. He touchingly pleads with them not to show him
any "unseasonable kindness" by averting the sentence of
death. In glowing language, which at times rises to exalted
lyrical heights, he declares his readiness to die for Christ and
thus prove himself an authentic "disciple." Christ's words
recorded in Matt. 10. 24 and Luke 14. 26 had evidently
made a deep impression on him. From Smyrna Ignatius was
taken to Troas in the north-west corner of Asia Minor, where
he wrote to the Philadelphians, the Smyrnaeans, and to the
bishop of the latter, Polycarp. He instructs the addressees
to send a delegation of prominent Christians to his beloved
Church at Antioch, where in the meantime the persecution
had come to an end and his flock enjoyed a period of peace.
From Troas he took ship for Neapolis, then passed through
Macedonia and Illyria, and after another voyage by sea probably landed at Brundisium, whence the rest of the journey
was made by land.

   There is no call here to expatiate upon the doctrinal value
of the Ignatian epistles. They must convey their own lessons
direct and fresh from the lips of their writer. Was Ignatius—
and the same query is applicable to Clement—a theologian?
Yes, and no. He was not a speculative theologian. He did
not, for example, bring the force of reason to bear upon the
great Christian Mysteries, as that of the Blessed Trinity, or
the Hypostatic Union. What he did was something more

substantial: he is a witness of the first rank to the actual teachings of historical Christianity. To keep these intact in their original purity is his chief endeavor; to warn against tampering with the body of Christian truth handed down by the Apostles, who in turn had received them from Christ— such was his main concern. His interest is in the *facts* of Christianity. Traditional Christianity—or, what John Henry Newman, when still an Anglican, called "the Catholic System"—is what Ignatius lived and died for. There is not a paragraph in his letters but reminds us of St. Paul's admonition to the Corinthians (1 Cor. 11. 2): "Uphold your traditions just as I have handed them on to you." This insistence on tradition gains new significance from the fact that the letters were written about A. D. 110, that is, only about fifteen or twenty years after the death of the last Apostle. Was this short space of time long enough to allow wholesale innovations to spread all over Asia Minor and take such firm root among the Christians that Ignatius could appeal to them as the traditions of the Apostles?[6] His whole concern is to safeguard the *depositum fidei* against the inroads of the two then rampant heresies, Judaism and Docetism.[7] The former is familiar to us from the writings of St. Paul. Ignatius's burning words are levelled against such converts from the Synagogue as continued to live "like Jews" after accepting the faith. A more subtle heresy was Docetism, which claimed that the human nature of Christ and, consequently, His birth, Passion, and Resurrection, were not real facts, but outright make-believes.

A word remains to be said about the tone of the subjoined English translation. The style of Ignatius[8] is so compact, so succinct, and so highly individual, that the reader of this translation who wishes to enjoy the additional luxury of tasting *all the Ignatian flavor* must of necessity go to the original. Translations are not made for the benefit of the scholar, but address themselves in the first place to a reader not conversant with the intricacies of Greek diction. What he looks for in taking up a translation is not merely accuracy, or fidelity to thought, but also readableness. He wants to know—of course in as few words as possible—what the Greek writer meant to say; he is anxious to grasp the sense without being compelled to turn to a footnote explaining it. A translation is, therefore, not deficient just because the number of its words exceeds that of the Greek. To give one illustration: In *Trallians* 4. 1, Ignatius says: Πολλὰ φρονῶ ἐν θεῷ. This is an extreme case of the general Greek, and the special Ignatian, penchant for brachylogy. To cling to the Greek wording and render: " I think many things in God," is to tax the reader with a puzzle. What Ignatius *means* to say is: "If I take God's view of things (for this sense of φρονῶ, see Mark 8. 33: " You do· not take God's view of things, but man's "), many thoughts pass through my mind." This is at once intelligible and smoothes the way for the next statement: " yet, I restrain myself " (" I do not allow myself to be puffed up," etc.). Note, also, in the sentence just quoted, Ignatius's passion for what seems to us an excessive straining of certain Greek prepositions; as, for example, ἐν. There is here, no doubt, an echo of St. Paul's favorite expression ἐν Χριστῷ: " in Christ "; that is, " in union with Christ "; " acting as a member of Christ's mystical body." Unfortunately for the translator, ἐν was capable also of several other pregnant uses. On the whole, it will be found, I trust, that, while I have emulated the Ignatian *brevitas*, I have avoided his *obscuritas*.

ᕀ   ᕀ   ᕀ

The text here used is that of F. X. Funk, revised by K. Bihlmeyer, *Die Apostolischen Väter*, 1. Teil (Tübingen 1924).

Other modern translations may be found in the following works, some of them mentioned in the Notes:

Krüger, G., in E. Hennecke's *Neutestamentliche Apokryphen* (2d ed., Tübingen 1924) 518-35.

Lake, K., *The Apostolic Fathers* 1 (Loeb Classical Library, London 1930).

Lightfoot, J. B., *The Apostolic Fathers. Part 2: S. Ignatius, S. Polycarp* 2 (London 1889).

Srawley, J. H., *The Epistles of St. Ignatius* (Society for Promoting Christian Knowledge, London 1935).

Zeller, F., *Die Apostolischen Väter* (Bibliothek der Kirchenväter, 2d ed., Kempten-Munich 1918).

For the *Epistle to the Trallians*, cf. also:

Moffatt, J., " An Approach to Ignatius," *Harv. Theol. Rev.* 29 (1936) 24-31.

IGNATIUS TO THE EPHESIANS

Ignatius, also called Theophorus, sends heartiest good wishes for unalloyed joy in Jesus Christ to the Church at Ephesus in Asia; a church deserving of felicitation, blessed, as she is, with greatness through the fullness of God the Father; predestined, before time was, to be—to her abiding and unchanging glory—forever united and chosen, through real suffering, by the will of the Father and Jesus Christ our God.[1]

1. With joy in God I welcomed your community, which possesses its dearly beloved name because of a right disposition,[2] enhanced by faith and love through Christ Jesus our Savior. Being imitators[3] of God, you have, once restored to new life in the Blood of God, perfectly accomplished the task so natural to you. 2 Indeed, as soon as you heard that I was coming from Syria in chains for our common Name and hope—hoping I might, thanks to your prayer, obtain the favor of fighting wild beasts at Rome and through this favor be able to prove myself a disciple[4]—you hastened to see me. 3 In the name of God, then, I have received your numerous community in the person of Onesimus,[5] a man of indescribable charity and your bishop here on earth.[6] I pray you in the spirit of Jesus Christ to love him, and wish all of you to resemble him. Blessed, indeed, is He whose grace made you worthy to possess such a bishop.[7]

2. As to my fellow servant[8] Burrus, your deacon by God's appointment and blessed with every gift, I wish he would stay at my side both for your honor and that of the bishop. But Crocus, too, a man of God and worthy of you, whom I received as a living example of your affection, has brought relief to me in every way; and I wish that the Father of Jesus Christ may comfort him in turn, as also Onesimus and Burrus and Euplus and Fronto, in whose persons I saw tokens of the affection of all of you. 2 May you ever be my joy, if indeed I deserve it! It is therefore proper in every way to glorify Jesus Christ who has glorified you, so that you, fully trained in unanimous submission, may be submissive to the bishop and the presbytery, and thus be sanctified in every respect.[9]

3. I give you no orders as though I were somebody. For, even though I am in chains for the sake of the Name,[10] I am not yet perfected in Jesus Christ. Indeed, I am now but being initiated into discipleship, and I address you as my fellow disciples.[11] Yes, I ought to be anointed[12] by you with faith, encouragement, patient endurance, and steadfastness. 2 However, since affection does not permit me to be silent when you are concerned, I am at once taking this opportunity to exhort you to live in harmony with the mind of God. Surely, Jesus Christ, our inseparable life,[13] for His part is the mind of the Father, just as the bishops, though appointed throughout the vast, wide earth,[14] represent for their part the mind of Jesus Christ.

4. Hence it is proper for you to act in agreement with the mind of the bishop; and this you do. Certain it is that your presbytery, which is a credit to its name, is a credit to God; for it harmonizes with the bishop as completely as the strings with a harp. This is why in the symphony of your concord and love the praises of Jesus Christ are sung. 2 But you, the rank and file,[15] should also form a choir, so that, joining the symphony by your concord, and by your unity taking your key note from God, you may with one voice through Jesus Christ sing a song to the Father. Thus He will both listen to you and by reason of your good life recognize in you the melodies [16] of His Son. It profits you, therefore, to continue in your flawless unity, that you may at all times have a share in God.

5. For a fact, if I in a short time became so warmly attached to your bishop—an attachment based not on human grounds but on spiritual [17]—how much more do I count you happy who are as closely knit to him as the Church is to Jesus Christ, and as Jesus Christ is to the Father! As a result, the symphony of unity is perfect. 2 Let no one deceive himself: unless a man is within the sanctuary, he has to go without *the Bread of God.*[18] Assuredly, if the prayer of one or two has such efficacy,[19] how much more that of the bishop and the entire Church! 3 It follows, then: he who absents himself from the common meeting, by that very fact shows pride and becomes a sectarian; for the Scripture says: [20] *God resists the proud.* Let us take care, therefore, not to oppose the bishop, that we may be submissive to God.

6. Furthermore: the more anyone observes that a bishop is discreetly silent, the more he should stand in fear of him.[21] Obviously, anyone whom the Master of the household puts in charge of His domestic affairs, ought to be received by us in the same spirit as He who has charged him with this duty. Plainly, then, one should look upon the bishop as upon the Lord Himself. 2 Now, Onesimus for his part overflows with praise of the good order that, thanks to God, exists in your midst. Truth is the rule of life for all of you, and heresy has no foothold among you. The fact is, you have nothing more to learn from anyone, since you listen [22] to Jesus Christ who speaks truthfully.

7. Some there are, you know, accustomed with vicious guile to go about with the Name on their lips, while they indulge in certain practices at variance with it and an insult to God. These you must shun as you would wild beasts: they are rabid dogs that bite in secret; you must beware of them, for they are hard to cure. 2 There is only one Physician, both carnal and spiritual,[23] born and unborn,[24] God become man, true life in death; sprung both from Mary and from God, first subject to suffering and then incapable of it—Jesus Christ Our Lord.

8. Let no one, then, deceive you, as indeed you are not being deceived, belonging wholly to God. For as long as no dissension calculated to plague you has taken firm root among you, it follows that you are leading a life conformable to God. Your lowliest servant,[25] I also consecrate myself to you Ephesians—that Church whose renown will go down the ages. 2 The carnal cannot live a spiritual life,[26] nor can the spiritual live a carnal life, any more than faith can act the part of infidelity, or infidelity the part of faith. But even the things you do in the flesh are spiritual, for you do all things in union with Jesus Christ.

9. I have heard of certain persons from elsewhere passing through, whose doctrine was bad. These you did not permit to sow their seed among you; you stopped your ears, so as not to receive the seed sown by them. You consider yourselves stones of the Father's temple, prepared for the edifice of God the Father, to be taken aloft by the hoisting engine of Jesus Christ, that is, the Cross, while the Holy Spirit serves you as

a rope; your faith is your spiritual windlass and your love the road which leads up to God. 2 And thus you all are fellow travellers, God-bearers and temple-bearers, Christ-bearers [27] and bearers of holiness, with the commandments of Jesus Christ for festal attire. At this I am jubilant, privileged as I am to converse with you through this letter, and to congratulate you because in your otherworldliness you love nothing but God alone.

10. But *pray unceasingly* [28] also for the rest of men, for they offer ground for hoping that they may be converted and win their way to God. Give them an opportunity therefore, at least by your conduct, of becoming your disciples. 2 Meet their angry outbursts with your own gentleness, their boastfulness with your humility, their revilings with your prayers, their error with *your constancy in the faith*, their harshness with your meekness; and beware of trying to match their example. 3 Let us prove ourselves their brothers through courtesy. Let us strive to follow the Lord's example and see who can suffer greater wrong, who more deprivation, who more contempt. Thus no weed of the devil will be found among you; but you will persevere in perfect chastity and sobriety through Jesus Christ, in body and soul. [29]

11. The last epoch has arrived! Therefore let us exercise restraint and fear lest God's long-suffering should turn to our condemnation. Obviously, we must either fear *the gathering storm of anger*, [30] or else cherish the present time of grace—one of the two; only let us be found in union with Christ Jesus so as to possess the true life. 2 Apart from Him, let nothing fascinate you. In union with Him I carry about these chains of mine—spiritual pearls they are! May I be privileged through your prayer—in which I wish I may ever have a share—to wear them when I rise from the dead! Thus I shall be found in the ranks of the Christians of Ephesus, who have ever been of one mind with the Apostles through the power of Jesus Christ.

12. I know who I am and to whom I am writing. I have been condemned, you have been spared; I am in danger, you are in perfect safety. 2 You are the highway[31] of God's martyrs. You are fellow initiates with Paul, a man sanctified, of character magnificently attested, and worthy of every felicitation, in whose footsteps I wish to be found when I come to meet God, and who in an entire epistle remembers you in Christ Jesus.

13. Make an effort, then, to meet more frequently to celebrate God's Eucharist and to offer praise.[32] For, when you meet frequently in the same place, the forces of Satan are overthrown, and his baneful influence is neutralized by the unanimity of your faith. 2 Peace is a precious thing: it puts an end to every war waged by heavenly or earthly enemies.

14. Nothing of this escapes you; only persevere to the end in your faith in, and your love for, Jesus Christ. Here is the beginning and the end of life: faith is the beginning, *the end is love;*[33] and when the two blend perfectly with each other, they are God.[34] Everything else that makes for right living is consequent upon these. 2 No one who professes faith sins;[35] no one who possesses love hates. *The tree is known by its fruit.*[36] In like manner, those who profess to belong to Christ will be known as such by their conduct. Certainly, what matters now is not mere profession of faith, but whether one is found to be actuated by it to the end.[37]

15. It is better to keep silence and be something than to talk and be nothing. Teaching is an excellent thing, provided the speaker practices what he teaches. Now, there is one Teacher who *spoke and it was done*.[88] But even what He did silently is worthy of the Father. 2 He who has made the words of Jesus really his own is able also to hear His silence. Thus he will be perfect: he will act through his speech and be understood through his silence. 3 Nothing is hidden from the Lord; no, even our secrets reach Him. Let us, then, do all things in the conviction that He dwells in us. Thus we shall be His temples and He will be our God within us.[89] And this is the truth, and it will be made manifest before our eyes. Let us, then, love Him as He deserves.

16. *Do not be deceived*, my brethren. Those who ruin homes *will not inherit the kingdom of God*.[40] 2 Now, if those who do this to gratify the flesh are liable to death, how much more a man who by evil doctrine ruins the faith in God, for which Jesus Christ was crucified! Such a filthy creature will go into the unquenchable fire, as will anyone that listens to him.

17. The Lord permitted myrrh to be poured on His head that He might breathe incorruption upon the Church. Do not let yourselves be anointed with the malodorous doctrine of the Prince of this world,[41] for fear he may carry you off into captivity—away from the life that is in store for you. 2 Why do we not all become wise, having received knowledge of God, that is, Jesus Christ! Why do we perish in folly, failing to appreciate the gift which the Lord has sent us in truth!

18. I offer my life's breath for the sake of the Cross, which is a stumbling block to the unbelievers,[42] but to us is salvation and eternal life. *What has become of the philosopher? What of the controversialist?* [43] What of the vaunting

of the so-called intellectuals? 2 The fact is, our God Jesus
Christ was conceived by Mary according to God's dispensa-
tion *of the seed of David*,⁴⁴ it is true, but also of the Holy
Spirit. He was born and was baptized, that by His Passion ⁴⁵
He might consecrate the water.

19. And the Prince of this world was in ignorance of the
virginity of Mary and her childbearing and also of the death
of the Lord—three mysteries loudly proclaimed to the world,
though accomplished in the stillness of God! ⁴⁶ 2 How, then,
were they revealed to the ages? A star blazed forth in the
sky, outshining all the other stars, and its light was indescribable, and its novelty provoked wonderment, and all the
starry orbs, with the sun and the moon, formed a choir round
that star; but its light exceeded that of all the rest, and there
was perplexity as to the cause of the unparalleled novelty.
3 This was the reason why every form of magic began to be
destroyed, every malignant spell to be broken, ignorance to be
dethroned, an ancient empire to be overthrown—God was
making His appearance in human form to mold *the newness*⁴⁷ of eternal life! Then at length was ushered in what
God had prepared in His counsels; then all the world was in
an upheaval because the destruction of death was being
prosecuted.

20. If Jesus Christ, yielding to your prayer, grants me the
favor and it is His will, I shall, in the subsequent letter which
I intend to write to you, still further explain the dispensation
which I have here only touched upon, regarding the New
Man Jesus Christ—a dispensation founded on faith in Him
and love for Him, on His Passion and Resurrection. 2 I will
do so especially if the Lord should reveal to me that you—the
entire community of you! ⁴⁸—are in the habit, through grace

derived from the Name, of meeting in common, animated by one faith and in union with Jesus Christ—who *in the flesh was of the line of David*,[49] the Son of Man and the Son of God—of meeting, I say, to show obedience with undivided mind to the bishop and the presbytery, and to break the same Bread,[50] which is the medicine of immortality,[51] the antidote against death, and everlasting life in Jesus Christ.

21. I offer my life as a ransom[52] for you and for those whom for the glory of God you sent to Smyrna, where, too, I am writing to you with thanks to the Lord and with love for Polycarp and you. Remember me, as may Jesus Christ remember you! 2 Pray for the Church in Syria, whence I am being led away in chains to Rome, though I am the least of the faithful there. But then, I was granted the favor of contributing to the honor of God. Farewell! May God the Father and Jesus Christ, *our common Hope*,[53] bless you!

IGNATIUS TO THE MAGNESIANS

Ignatius, also called Theophorus, to the Church at Magnesia by the Maeander, a church blessed with the grace of God the Father through Jesus Christ our Savior, in whom I salute her. Heartiest greetings and good wishes to her in[1] God the Father and in Jesus Christ.

1. When I learned of your well-ordered[2] God-inspired love, I was jubilant and decided to have a chat with you in the spirit of the faith in[3] Jesus Christ. 2 I am privileged to bear a name[4] radiant with divine splendor, and so in the chains which I carry about on me, I sing the praises of the Churches and pray for union in their midst, a union based on the flesh and spirit[5] of Jesus Christ, our enduring life; a union based on faith and love—the greatest blessing;[6] and, most especially, a union with Jesus and the Father.[7] If in this union we patiently endure all the abuse of the Prince of this world and escape unscathed, we shall happily make our way to God.[8]

2. Now, then, it has been my privilege to have a glimpse of you all in the person of Damas, your bishop[9] and a man of God, and in the persons of your worthy presbyters Bassus and Apollonius, and of my fellow servant,[10] the deacon Zotion. Would that I might enjoy the latter's company! He is obedient to the bishop as[11] to the grace of God, and to the presbyters as to the law of Jesus Christ.

3. But for you, too, it is fitting not to take advantage of the bishop's youth, but rather, because he embodies the authority of God the Father, to show him every mark of respect—and your presbyters, so I learn, are doing just that: they do not seek to profit by his youthfulness, which strikes the bodily eye;[12] no, they are wise in God[13] and therefore defer to him—or, rather, not to him, but to the Father of Jesus Christ, the bishop of all men. 2 So, then, for the honor of Him who has deigned[14] to choose us, it is proper to obey without any hypocrisy. It is not really that a man deceives this particular bishop who is visible, but tries to overreach Him who is invisible. When this happens, his reckoning is not with man,[15] but with God who knows what is secret.

4. The proper thing, then, is not merely to be styled Christians,[15a] but also to be such—just as there are those who style a man bishop, but completely disregard him in their conduct. Such persons do not seem to me to have a good conscience, inasmuch as they do not assemble in the fixed order[16] prescribed by him.

5. Now, as all things have an end, and those two issues, death and life, are set before us at one and the same time, so each man is bound to go to his own place.[17] 2 It is the same as with two coinages, the one of God, the other of the world; and each of them has its own stamp impressed upon it: the unbelievers bear the stamp of this world, while the believers, animated by love, bear the stamp of God the Father through Jesus Christ, whose life is not in us unless we are ready of our own accord to die in order[18] to share in His Passion.

6. Since, then, in the persons mentioned before I have with the eyes of the faith looked upon your whole community and have come to love it, I exhort you to strive to do all things in harmony with God: the bishop is to preside[19]

in the place of God, while the presbyters are to function as the council of the Apostles, and the deacons, who are most dear to me, are entrusted with the ministry of Jesus Christ, who before time began was with the Father and has at last [20] appeared. 2 Conform yourselves, then—all of you—to God's ways, and respect one another, and let no one regard his neighbor with the eyes of the flesh,[21] but love one another at all times in Jesus Christ. Let there be nothing among you tending to divide you, but be united with the bishop and those who preside—serving at once as a pattern and as a lesson of incorruptibility.

7. Just as the Lord, therefore, being one with the Father, did nothing without Him,[22] either by Himself, or through the Apostles, so neither must you undertake anything without the bishop and the presbyters; nor must you attempt to convince yourselves that anything you do on your own account [23] is acceptable. No; at your meetings there must be one prayer, one supplication, one mind, one hope in love, in joy that is flawless, that is [24] Jesus Christ, who stands supreme. 2 Come together, all of you, as to one temple and one altar, to one Jesus Christ—to Him who came forth from one Father and yet remained with, and returned to, one.[25]

8. *Do not be led astray* [26] by those erroneous teachings and ancient fables which are utterly worthless. Indeed, if at this date we still conform to Judaism, then we own that we have not received grace. 2 Why, the Prophets, those men so very near to God, lived in conformity with Christ Jesus.[27] This, too, was the reason why they were persecuted, inspired as they were by His grace to bring full conviction to an unbelieving world that there is one God, who manifested Himself through Jesus Christ, His Son—who, being His

Word, came forth out of the silence into the world [28] and won the full approval of Him whose Ambassador He was.

9. Consequently, if the people who were given to obsolete practices faced the hope of a new life, and if these no longer observe the Sabbath, but regulate their calendar by the Lord's Day, the day, too, on which our Life rose by His power and through the medium of His death—though some deny this; and if to this mystery we owe our faith and because of it submit to sufferings to prove ourselves disciples of Jesus Christ, our only Teacher: 2 how, then, can we possibly live apart from Him of whom, by the working of the Spirit, even the Prophets were disciples and to whom they looked forward as their Teacher? And so He, for whom they rightly waited, came and raised them from the dead.

10. Let us not, then, be insensible to His loving kindness. Certainly, if He were to imitate our way of acting, we should be done for instantly. We must, therefore, prove ourselves His disciples and learn to live like Christians. Assuredly, whoever is called by a name other than this,[29] is not of God. 2 Hence, put away the deteriorated leaven, a leaven stale and sour, and turn to the new leaven, that is, Jesus Christ. Be salted in Him [30] to keep any among you from being spoiled, for by your odor you will be tested. 3 It is absurd to have Jesus Christ on the lips, and at the same time live like a Jew. No; Christianity did not believe in Judaism, but Judaism believed in Christianity, and in its bosom was assembled *everyone professing* [31] faith in God.

11. Now this, dearly beloved, I do not write as though I had learned that any of you were men of that description, but because, as one who is not your superior,[32] I merely wish to warn you betimes not to yield to the bait of false doctrine, but to believe most steadfastly in the birth, the Passion, and the Resurrection,[33] which took place during the procuratorship of Pontius Pilate. Facts these are, real and established by Jesus Christ, *our hope.*[34] May God grant that none of you may relinquish it!

12. May you be my joy in all respects, if indeed I deserve it! For, though I am in chains, compared with one of you who are free, I am nothing. I know that you are not conceited, for you have Jesus Christ in you. What is more, I know that when I praise you, you blush, just as the Scripture says: [35] *The just man is his own accuser.*

13. Be zealous, therefore, to stand squarely on the decrees of the Lord and the Apostles, *that in all things whatsoever you may prosper,*[36] in body and in soul, in faith and in love, in the Son and the Father and the Spirit, in the beginning and the end, together with your most reverend bishop and with your presbytery—that fittingly woven spiritual crown![37] —and with your deacons, men of God. 2 Submit to the bishop and to each other's rights, just as did Jesus Christ in the flesh[38] to the Father, and as the Apostles did to Christ and the Father and the Spirit, so that there may be oneness both of flesh and of spirit.

14. Knowing that you are steeped in God,[39] I am exhorting you but briefly. Remember me in your prayers that I may happily make my way to God. Remember, too, the Church in Syria, of which I am an unworthy member. Yes, I do stand in need of your God-inspired prayer and your love. Thus the Church in Syria will be privileged through your Church to be quickened with refreshing dew.

15. The Ephesians at Smyrna—the place from which I am writing to you—send their greetings. Like yourselves, they have come here for the glory of God. They have revived my spirits in every way, as does Polycarp, the bishop of Smyrna. The rest of the Churches, too, beg to be remembered in honor of Jesus Christ. Farewell—you who, being of one mind with God, possess an unflinching [40] spirit—which is to be like Jesus Christ.

IGNATIUS TO THE TRALLIANS

Ignatius, also called Theophorus, to the holy Church at Tralles in Asia, loved by God the Father of Jesus Christ; elect and an honor to God; enjoying inward and outward peace[1] through the Passion of Jesus Christ, who is our hope when we rise to be with Him.[2] I salute her in Apostolic fashion[3] with the fullness[4] of grace and offer her heartiest good wishes.

1. Beyond reproach, I hear, and unshaken[5] in patient endurance is your disposition—not an acquired habit, but a natural endowment. I was informed of it by Polybius, your bishop, who by the will of God and Jesus Christ came to Smyrna and so heartily shared my joy at the chains which I bear in Christ Jesus,[6] that in his person I beheld your whole community. 2 Welcoming, then, your God-inspired goodwill, I burst into thanks and praise, finding that you, as I learned, were patterning yourselves after God.[7]

2. Surely, when you submit to the bishop as representing Jesus Christ, it is clear to me that you are not living the life of men,[8] but that of Jesus Christ, who died for us, that through faith in His death you might escape dying. 2 It is needful, then—and such is your practice—that you do nothing without[9] your bishop; but be subject also to the presbytery as representing the Apostles of Jesus Christ, *our hope*,[10] in whom we are expected to live forever.[11] 3 It is further necessary that the deacons, the dispensers of the mysteries[12] of

75

Jesus Christ, should win the approval of all in every way; for they are not dispensers of food and drink, but ministers of a church of God. Hence they must be on their guard against criticism, as against fire.

3. Likewise, let all respect the deacons as representing Jesus Christ, the bishop as a type[13] of the Father, and the presbyters as God's high council and as the Apostolic college.[14] Apart from these, no church deserves the name.[15] 2 In these matters I am convinced that such is your attitude; for I have received, and have with me, the embodiment of your affection in the person of your bishop. His very demeanor is a powerful sermon, his gentleness a mighty influence—a man whom even the unbelievers, I am sure, respect. 3 From love for you I spare your feelings—though I might write more sternly in this regard. But I do not think that I, a man condemned, should give you orders like an Apostle.

4. Many thoughts are mine when I take God's view of things;[16] yet I keep within due bounds, that I may not perish through boastfulness. Right now I must fear the more, and pay no heed to those who flatter my vanity.[17] Really, those who speak to me in this strain torture me. 2 True, I am in love with suffering,[18] but I do not know if I deserve the honor.[19] My passionate longing is not manifest to many, but it grips me all the more.[20] What I need is equanimity, by which the Prince of this world[21] is undone.

5. Am I not able to write to you about heavenly things? I am; but I fear to inflict harm on you who are mere babes.[22] Pardon me, then[23]—you must not be choked by what you cannot assimilate. 2 It is the same with me: just because I am in chains and able to grasp heavenly things—the ranks of the angels, the hierarchy of principalities, *things visible and* *invisible* [24]—it does not immediately follow that I am a disciple. Plainly, we are yet short of much if we are not to be short of God.[25]

6. I exhort you therefore—no, not I, but the love of Jesus Christ: partake of Christian food exclusively; abstain from plants of alien growth, that is, heresy. 2 Heretics [26] weave Jesus Christ into their web—to win our confidence, just like persons who administer a deadly drug mixed with honeyed wine, which the unsuspecting gladly take—and with baneful relish they swallow death!

7. So, then, beware of such! And you will do so if you are not puffed up and cling inseparably to God Jesus Christ, to the bishop, and to the precepts of the Apostles. 2 He that is inside the sanctuary is pure; he that is outside the sanctuary is not pure. In other words: he that does anything apart [27] from bishop, presbytery, or deacon has no pure conscience.

8. Not that I have discovered any such thing in your midst; no, I merely warn you betimes since you are dear to me and I foresee the devil's snares. Take up the practice, then, of kind forbearance and renew yourselves in faith, which is the Flesh [28] of the Lord, and in love, which is the Blood of Jesus Christ. 2 Let none of you bear a grudge against his neighbor. Give no pretext to the pagans, so that, because of a few foolish persons, God's own people may not be reviled. For *woe unto him through whom my name is reviled among some out of folly.*[29]

9. Stop your ears therefore when anyone speaks to you that stands apart from Jesus Christ, from David's scion and Mary's Son, who was really born [30] and ate and drank, really persecuted by Pontius Pilate, really crucified and died while heaven and earth and the underworld looked on; 2 who also

really rose from the dead, since His Father raised Him up,—
His Father, who will likewise raise us also who believe in
Him through Jesus Christ, apart from whom we have no
real life.

10. But if, as some atheists, that is, unbelievers, say, His
suffering was but a make-believe—when, in reality, they
themselves are make-believes—then why am I in chains?
Why do I even pray that I may fight wild beasts? In vain,
then, do I die! My testimony is, after all, but a lie about the
Lord! [81]

11. Shun these wildlings, then, which bear but deadly
fruit, and when one tastes it, he is outright doomed to die!
Surely, such persons are not *the planting of the Father.*[82]
2 For if they were, they would appear as branches of the
Cross, and their fruit would be imperishable—the Cross
through which by His Passion He calls you to Him, being
members of His body. Evidently, no head can be born
separately, without members, since God means[83] complete
oneness, which is Himself.

12. I greet you from Smyrna together with the Churches
of God present here with me. They comfort me in every way,
both in body and in soul. 2 My chains, which I carry about
on me for Jesus Christ, begging that I may happily make my
way to God, exhort you: persevere in your concord and in
your community prayers. It is certainly fitting for you individually, but especially for the presbyters, to give comfort to
the bishop in honor of the Father and Jesus Christ and the
Apostles. 3 I beg you to listen to me in love, so that I may
not, by writing to you, prove witness against you. But also
pray for me, who stand in need of your charity before the
mercy seat of God. Thus I shall be granted that portion on

the obtaining of which my heart is set,[34] and shall not be found a reprobate.

13. The love of the Smyrnaeans[35] and the Ephesians sends you greetings. Remember in your prayers the Church in Syria, to which I do not deserve to belong, being the least of her members. 2 Farewell in the name of Jesus Christ. Be obedient to the bishop as to the commandment, and so, too, to the presbytery. And love one another, man for man,[36] with undivided heart. 3 My spirit is consecrated to you, not only now, but also when I have happily made my way to God. For I am still in danger. But then, the Father is faithful and will, in Jesus Christ, answer both my and your prayer. May you in union with Him be found above reproach.

IGNATIUS TO THE ROMANS

Ignatius, also called Theophorus, to the Church that has found mercy[1] in the transcendent Majesty of the Most High Father and of Jesus Christ, His only Son; the church by the will of Him who willed all things that exist, beloved and illuminated through[2] the faith and love of Jesus Christ our God; which also presides in the chief place of the Roman territory; a church worthy of God, worthy of honor, worthy of felicitation, worthy of praise, worthy of success, worthy of sanctification, and presiding in love, maintaining the law of Christ, and bearer of the Father's name: her do I therefore salute in the name of Jesus Christ, the Son of the Father. Heartiest good wishes for unimpaired joy in Jesus Christ our God, to those who are united in flesh and spirit[3] by every commandment of His; who imperturbably enjoy the full measure of God's grace and have every foreign stain filtered out of them.

1. By prayer to God I have obtained the favor of seeing your venerable faces;[4] in fact, I have been pleading for an even greater favor: as a prisoner in Christ Jesus I hope to embrace you, provided it is His will that I should be privileged to reach the goal. 2 An auspicious beginning has certainly been made—if only I obtain[5] the grace of taking due possession of my inheritance without hindrance. The truth is, I am afraid it is your love[6] that will do me wrong. For you, of course, it is easy to achieve your object; but for me it is difficult to win my way to God, should you be wanting in consideration for me.

2. Surely, I do not want you *to court the good pleasure of men*,[7] but to please God, as indeed you do please Him. Yes, I shall never again have such an opportunity of winning my way to God, nor can you, if you remain quiet, ever have your name inscribed[8] on a more glorious achievement. For, if you quietly ignore me, I am the word of God;[9] but if you fall in love with my human nature, I shall, on the contrary, be a mere sound. 2 Grant me no more than that you let my blood be spilled in sacrifice[10] to God, while yet there is an altar ready. You should form a choir of love and sing a song to the Father through Jesus Christ, because God has graciously summoned the bishop of Syria to come from the rising of the sun to the setting. How glorious to be a setting sun— away from the world, on to God! May I rise in His presence![11]

3. You have never grudged any man. You have taught others. All I want is that the lessons you inculcate in initiating disciples remain in force.[12] 2 Only beg for me strength within and without, that I may be a man not merely of words, but also of resolution. In this way I shall not only be called a Christian, but also prove to be one. For if I prove to be one, I can also be called a true believer even then when I am no longer seen by the world.[13] 3 Nothing that is seen is good. Our God Jesus Christ certainly is the more clearly seen now that He is in the Father. Whenever Christianity is hated by the world, what counts is not power of persuasion, but greatness.[14]

4. I am writing to all the Churches and state emphatically to all that I die willingly for God, provided you do not interfere. I beg you, do not show me unseasonable kindness. Suffer me to be the food of wild beasts, which are the means of my making my way to God. God's wheat I am, and by the teeth of wild beasts I am to be ground that I may prove Christ's pure bread. 2 Better still, coax the wild beasts to become my tomb and to leave no part of my person behind: once I have fallen asleep, I do not wish to be a burden to anyone. Then only shall I be a genuine disciple of Jesus Christ when the world will not see even my body. Petition Christ in my behalf that through these instruments I may prove God's sacrifice. 3 Not like Peter and Paul do I issue any orders to you. They were Apostles,[15] I am a convict; they were free, I am until this moment a slave. But once I have suffered, I shall become a freedman of Jesus Christ, and, united with Him, I shall rise a free man. Just now I learn, being in chains, to desire nothing.

5. All the way from Syria to Rome I am fighting wild beasts, on land and sea, by day and night, chained as I am to ten leopards, that is, a detachment of soldiers, who prove themselves the more malevolent for kindnesses shown them. Yet in the school of this abuse I am more and more trained in discipleship, *although I am not therefore justified.*[16] 2 Oh, may the beasts prepared for me be my joy! And I pray that they may be found to be ready for me. I will even coax them to make short work of me, not as has happened to some whom they were too timid to touch. And should they be unwilling to attack me who am willing, I will myself compel them. 3 Pardon me—I know very well where my advantage lies. At last I am well on the way to being a disciple. May nothing *seen or unseen,*[17] fascinate me, so that I may happily make my way to Jesus Christ! Fire, cross, struggles with wild beasts, wrenching of bones, mangling of limbs, crunching of the whole body, cruel tortures inflicted by the devil—let them come upon me, provided[18] only I make my way to Jesus Christ.

6. Of no use [19] to me will be the farthest reaches of the universe or the kingdoms of this world. *I would rather die* [20] and come to Jesus Christ than be king over the entire earth. Him I seek who died for us; Him I love who rose again because of us. The birth pangs are upon me. 2 Forgive me, brethren; do not obstruct my coming to life—do not wish me to die; do not make a gift to the world of one who wants to be God's. Beware of seducing me with matter; suffer me to receive pure light. Once arrived there, I shall be a man. 3 Permit me to be an imitator of my suffering God. [21] If anyone holds Him in his heart, let him understand what I am aspiring to; and then let him sympathize with me, knowing in what distress I am.

7. The Prince of this world is resolved to abduct me, and to corrupt my Godward aspirations. Let none of you, therefore, who will then be present, assist him. Rather, side with me, that is, with God. Do not have Jesus Christ on your lips, and the world in your hearts. 2 Give envy no place among you. And should I upon my arrival plead for your intervention, do not listen to me. Rather, give heed to what I write to you. I am writing while still alive, but my yearning is for death. My Love [22] has been crucified, and I am not on fire with the love of earthly things. But there is in me a *Living Water*, [23] which is eloquent and within me says: " Come to the Father." 3 I have no taste for corruptible food or for the delights of this life. *Bread of God* [24] is what I desire; that is, the Flesh of Jesus Christ, *who was of the seed of David;* [25] and for my drink I desire His Blood, that is, incorruptible love.

8. No longer do I wish to live after the manner of men; [26] and this is what will happen if you wish it so. Wish it, that your own wishes, too, may be fulfilled. 2 By this short letter I beseech you: do believe me! Jesus Christ will make it clear to you that I speak the truth—He on whose lips there are no lies, through whom the Father has spoken truthfully. 3 Pray for me that I may succeed. What I write to you does not please the appetites of the flesh, but it pleases the mind of God. If I suffer, you have loved me; if I am rejected, you have hated me!

9. Remember in your prayers the Church in Syria, which now has God for her Shepherd in my stead. Jesus Christ alone will be her Bishop, together with your love.[27] 2 For myself, I am ashamed to be counted as one of her members. I certainly do not deserve to be one, being the least of them and one that came to birth unexpectedly. However, if I but make my way to God, then by His mercy I shall be someone. 3 My spirit salutes you, and so does the affection of the Churches that offered their hospitality to me, not as to a chance visitor, but in deference to Jesus Christ. Why, even those not adjoining my route—the route by which my body travelled—hastened in advance from town after town to meet me.

10. I am sending [28] you this letter from Smyrna through the kindness of the Ephesians, who deserve so much praise. Among many others Crocus is here with me—a dearly beloved name to me! 2 As to the men from Syria who for the glory of God have gone to Rome to meet you there, you have, I trust, made their acquaintance. Please, inform them also that I am near. One and all they are men of God and will be an honor to you. You will do well to give them every comfort. 3 I am writing this to you on the 24th of August. Farewell to the end in the patient endurance [29] of Jesus Christ.

IGNATIUS TO THE PHILADELPHIANS

Ignatius, also called Theophorus, to the Church of God the Father and the Lord Jesus Christ, which is at Philadelphia in Asia; a church which has found mercy and is irrevocably of one mind with God; which unwaveringly exults in the Passion of Our Lord, and firmly believes in His Resurrection through sheer mercy. This Church I salute in the Blood of Jesus Christ. She is a source of everlasting joy, especially when the members are at one with the bishop and his assistants, the presbyters and deacons, that have been appointed in accordance with the wish of Jesus Christ, and whom He has, by His own will, through the operation of His Holy Spirit, confirmed in loyalty.

1. Regarding this bishop I am informed that he holds the supreme office in the community not by his own efforts,[1] or by men's doing, or for personal glory. No, he holds it by the love of God the Father and the Lord Jesus Christ. I am charmed[2] with his sweetness of manner. He accomplishes more by his silence than others that talk to no purpose. 2 No wonder; he is as perfectly in accord with the commandments as strings are with a harp. With all my heart, therefore, I laud his disposition[3] to please God, a disposition virtuous and perfect, as I am very well aware; his unshaken constancy, too, and his passionless temper, modelled on the transcendent gentleness of the living God.[4]

2. *Being born*, then, *of the light* of truth,[5] shun division

85

and bad doctrines. Where the shepherd is, there you, being sheep, must follow.⁶ 2 For, many wolves there are, apparently worthy of confidence, who with the bait of baneful pleasure seek to capture the runners in God's race; ⁷ but if you stand united, they will have no success.

3. Avoid the noxious weeds. Their gardener is not Jesus Christ, because they are not the planting of the Father.⁸ Not that I found any division in your midst; but I did find that there had been a purge. 2 Surely, all those that belong to God and Jesus Christ are the very ones that side with the bishop; and all those that may yet change their mind and return to the unity of the Church, will likewise belong to God, and thus lead a life acceptable to Jesus Christ. 3 *Do not be deceived*, my brethren: ⁹ if a man runs after a schismatic, *he will not inherit the Kingdom of God*; if a man chooses to be a dissenter, he severs all connection with the Passion.

4. Take care, then, to partake of one Eucharist; ¹⁰ for, one is the Flesh of Our Lord Jesus Christ, and one the cup to unite us with His Blood, and one altar, just as there is one bishop assisted by the presbytery and the deacons, my fellow servants.¹¹ Thus you will conform in all your actions to the will of God.

5. My brethren, my love for you overflows all bounds, and it is my supreme delight to provide you with safeguards, though it is really not I that do it, but Jesus Christ. Being in chains for His sake, I am all the more apprehensive, since I am not yet perfected. But then, your prayer will make me perfect in the sight of God, so that I may win the lot which, through mercy, has fallen to me. I take refuge in the Gospel, which to me is Jesus in the flesh, and in the Apostles, as represented by the presbytery of the Church.[12] 2 But let us also cherish the Prophets, because they, for their part, foreshadowed the Gospel; and they hoped in Him and waited for Him and were saved by their belief in Him; for thus they were one with Jesus Christ. O those lovable and wonderful saints! Their merits are attested by Jesus Christ, and their message is part and parcel of the Gospel of our common hope.[13]

6. But should anyone expound Judaism, do not listen to him. It is preferable, surely, to listen to a circumcized man preaching Christianity than to an uncircumcized man preaching Judaism. But if neither of them preaches Jesus Christ, they are to me tombstones and graves of the dead,[14] on which only the names of the dead are inscribed. 2 Shun, then, the base artifices and snares of the Prince of this world, for fear you may be harassed by his scheming and grow weak in your love. Rather, come together, all of you, with undivided heart. 3 I thank my God that I have a good conscience as concerning you, and that no one has occasion to boast that I was a burden to anyone [15] either secretly or openly, in great matters or in small. But I also pray for all those in whose midst I spoke, that they may not find in my words any testimony against them.

7. For, even though some were willing enough to lead my human spirit into error, yet the Spirit is not led into error, since He proceeds from God. Indeed, *He knows where He comes from and whither He goes,*[16] and lays bare what is secret.[17] I cried out, while in your midst, and said in a ringing voice—God's voice: "Give heed to the bishop and to the presbytery and to the deacons." 2 Some, however, suspected I was saying this because I had previous knowledge of the

7 1

division caused by some; but He for whose sake I am in chains is my witness, that I had not learned it from any human source.[18] No, it was the Spirit who kept preaching in these words: " Apart from the bishop do nothing; preserve your persons as shrines of God; cherish unity, shun divisions; do as Jesus Christ did,[19] for He, too, did as the Father did."

8. I was doing my part, therefore, acting as a man trained to cherish unity. Where there is division and passion, there is no place for God. Now, the Lord forgives all if they change their mind and by this change of mind return to union with God and the council of the bishop. I trust in the grace of Jesus Christ, who will free you from all enslavement.[20] 2 I exhort you never to act in a spirit of factiousness, but according to what you learnt in the school of Christ. When I heard some say, " Unless I find it in the official records—in the Gospel I do not believe ";[21] and when I answered them, " It is in the Scriptures," they retorted: " That is just the point at issue." But to me the official record is Jesus Christ; the inviolable record is His Cross and His death and His Resurrection and the faith of which He is the Author. These are the things which, thanks to your prayer, I want to be my justification.

9. Good, too, are priests; but better is the High Priest who was entrusted with the Holy of Holies, who alone was entrusted with the hidden designs of God. He is *the door* [22] of the Father, through which enter Abraham and Isaac and Jacob and the Prophets and the Apostles and the Church. All these [23] are means of being united with God. 2 But the Gospel contains something special—the Advent of the Savior Our Lord Jesus Christ, His Passion and His Resurrection. The beloved Prophets announced His coming, whereas the

Gospel is the imperishable fulfillment. All things alike are good, provided your faith is rooted in love.

10. Since it was reported to me that—thanks to your prayer and kindly interest,[24] inspired by Jesus Christ—the Church at Antioch in Syria is at peace, it is proper that you, as a church of God, should appoint a deacon to go there as God's ambassador, and congratulate the people in a public meeting, and give glory to the Name.[25] 2 Blessed in Jesus Christ is he who is to discharge this office; and you, too, will reap glory. If only you are determined, it is not impossible to do this for God's name, just as the neighboring Churches have, some of them, delegated bishops—others, presbyters and deacons.

11. Now, as to Philo, the deacon from Cilicia, a man of attested merit, who even now assists me in the ministry of the word of God together with Rheus Agathopus, an exquisite character, who has been accompanying me from Syria after turning his back upon this life—well, both these men testify (and I, too, thank God on your behalf) that you received them kindly. May the Lord do so to you! As for those who treated them with disrespect, may they be redeemed by the grace of Jesus Christ! 2 In their love[26] the brethren of Troas wish to be remembered. It is from here that I send this letter through the kindness of Burrus, who, as a testimonial of honor, was sent by the Ephesians and Smyrnaeans to accompany me. These men will be honored by the Lord Jesus Christ, in whom they hope with body and soul and spirit and faith and love and concord. Farewell in Jesus Christ, *our common Hope*.[27]

IGNATIUS TO THE SMYRNAEANS

Ignatius, also called Theophorus, to the Church of God the Father and the beloved Jesus Christ; a church mercifully endowed with every gift; overflowing with faith and love;[1] lacking in no gift;[2] radiant with God's splendor, and fruitful mother of saints.[3] To the Church at Smyrna[4] in Asia I send best wishes for irreproachableness of sentiment and loyalty to the word of God.

1. I extol Jesus Christ, the God who has granted you such wisdom. For I have observed that you are thoroughly trained in unshaken faith, being nailed, as it were, to the Cross of the Lord Jesus Christ both in body and in soul,[5] and that you are well established in love through the Blood of Christ and firmly believe in Our Lord: He is really *of the line of David according to the flesh,*[6] and the Son of God by the will and power of God; was really born of a virgin, and baptized by John *in order to comply with every ordinance.*[7] 2 Under Pontius Pilate and the tetrarch Herod He was really[8] nailed to the cross in the flesh for our sake—of whose fruit we are, in virtue of His most blessed Passion. And thus, through the Resurrection, *He raised a banner*[9] for all times for His saints and faithful followers, whether among the Jews or the Gentiles, that they might be united in a single body, that is, His Church.[10]

2. All these sufferings, assuredly, He underwent for our sake, that we might be saved. And He suffered really, as He also really raised Himself from the dead.[11] It is not as some unbelievers say, who maintain that His suffering was a make-believe.[12] In reality, it is they that are make-believes: and, as their notion, so their end: they will be bodiless and ghost-like shapes![13]

3. For myself, I know and believe that He was in the flesh even after the Resurrection. 2 And when He came to Peter and Peter's companions, He said to them: "*Here; feel me and see that I am not a bodiless ghost.*"[14] Immediately they touched Him and, through this contact with His Flesh and Spirit, believed. For the same reason they despised death and, in fact, proved stronger than death. 3 Again, after the Resurrection, He ate and drank with them[15] like a being of flesh and blood, though spiritually[16] one with the Father.

4. I am urging these things on you, beloved, although I know that you are of the same mind. I am cautioning you betimes, however, against wild beasts in human form, whom you ought not only not to receive, but, if possible, even avoid meeting. Only pray for them, if somehow they may change their mind[17]—a difficult thing! But that is in the power of Jesus Christ, our true Life. 2 Surely, if those things were done by Our Lord as a mere make-believe, then I in my chains, too, am a make-believe! Why, moreover, did I surrender myself to death, to fire, to the sword, to wild beasts? Well, to be near the sword is to be near God; to be in the claws of wild beasts is to be in the hands of God. Only let it be done in the name of Jesus Christ! To suffer with Him I endure all things,[18] if He, who became perfect man,[19] gives me the strength.[20]

5. Some disown Him through ignorance, or, rather, were disowned by Him, being advocates of death rather than the

1. They were not convinced by the prophecies or by the Law of Moses; no, not even to this day by the Gospel or the sufferings of our own people; [21] 2 for they entertain the same view of us. Really, what good does anyone do me if he praises me, but blasphemes my Lord by not admitting that He carried living flesh about Him? [22] He who does not admit this, has absolutely disowned Him, and what he carries about him is a corpse. 3 Their names—names of unbelievers they are!—I do not think advisable to write down. In fact, I even wish I did not remember them, until they change their mind concerning the Passion, which is our resurrection.

6. Let no one be deceived! [23] Even the heavenly powers and the angels in their splendor and the principalities, both *visible and invisible*, [24] must either believe in the Blood of Christ, or else face damnation. *Let him grasp it who can.* [25] Let no rank [26] puff up anyone; for faith and love are paramount—the greatest blessings in the world. 2 Observe those who hold erroneous opinions concerning the grace of Jesus Christ which has come to us, and see how they run counter to the mind of God! They concern themselves with neither works of charity, nor widows, nor orphans, nor the distressed, nor those in prison or out of it, nor the hungry or thirsty.

7. From Eucharist and prayer they hold aloof, because they do not confess that the Eucharist is the Flesh of our Savior Jesus Christ, [27] which suffered for our sins, and which the Father in His loving-kindness raised from the dead. And so, those who question *the gift of God* [28] perish in their contentiousness. It would be better for them to have love, so as to share in the resurrection. 2 It is proper, therefore, to avoid associating with such people and not to speak about them either in private or in public, but to study the Prophets attentively and, especially, the Gospel, in which the Passion is revealed to us and the Resurrection shown in its fulfillment. Shun division as the beginning of evil.

8. You must all follow the lead of the bishop, as Jesus Christ followed that of the Father; follow the presbytery as you would the Apostles; reverence the deacons as you would God's commandment. Let no one do anything touching the Church, apart from the bishop. Let that celebration of the Eucharist be considered valid which is held under the bishop or anyone to whom he has committed it. 2 Where the bishop appears, there let the people be, just as where Jesus Christ is, there is the Catholic Church.[29] It is not permitted without authorization from the bishop either to baptize or to hold an agape;[30] but whatever he approves is also pleasing to God. Thus everything you do will be *proof against danger and valid.*[31]

9. It is consonant with reason, therefore, that we should come to our senses, while we still have time to change our ways and turn to God. It is well to revere God and bishop. He who honors a bishop is honored by God. He who does anything without the knowledge of the bishop worships the devil. 2 May all things, then, be yours in abundance through grace, for you deserve it. You have brought relief to me in every respect, and may Jesus Christ do so to you! Whether I was absent or present, you have shown me love. Your reward is God, to whom you will come if you endure all things for His sake.

10. As to Philo and Rheus Agathopus, who accompanied me in the name of God, it was good of you to give them a warm reception as to servants of Christ God. For their part, they thank the Lord on your behalf, because you offered them every comfort. In no respect—that is certain!—will you be losers. 2 A ransom for you are my life and my chains, which you did not despise and of which you were not ashamed.[32] Neither will Jesus Christ, our consummate hope, be ashamed of you.

11. Your prayer made its way to the Church at Antioch in Syria. Coming from there in chains radiant with divine splendor, I send greetings to all. Not that I deserve to belong to that community, being the least of its members; but by the will (of God) I was granted this favor—no, not because of any conscious deed, but because of the grace of God. Would that this grace were given me in perfection, that through your prayer I may make my way to God! 2 Now, that your own work may be made perfect both on earth and in heaven, it is proper, for the honor of God, that your Church should send a God-empowered delegate to go to Syria and congratulate the people on enjoying peace, having recovered their normal greatness, and having their full status restored to them.[33] 3 It therefore appears to me to be a God-inspired undertaking to send one of your number with a letter for the purpose of joining in the celebration of their God-given tranquillity, and because they have, thanks to your prayer, at last made port. Be perfect, therefore, and devise a perfect method. You need only be willing to do well, and God is ready to assist you.

12. In their affection[34] the brethren at Troas wish to be remembered to you. It is from here that I send this letter through the kindness of Burrus, whom you conjointly with your brethren, the Ephesians, commissioned to accompany me. He has given me every possible comfort. And would that all might imitate him, for he is a pattern of what a minister of God should be. God's grace will reward him in every way. 2 Greetings to the bishop, that man of God, to the God-minded presbytery, to the deacons my fellow servants, to the whole community, individually and collectively, in the name of Jesus Christ, in His Flesh and Blood, in His Passion and Resurrection, both corporal and spiritual, in unity with God and with you. Grace be to you and mercy and peace and patient endurance forever.

13. Greetings to the families of my brethren, including their wives and children, and to the virgins who are enrolled among the widows.[85] Farewell in the power of the Father! Philo, who is with me, wishes to be remembered to you. 2 Offer my respects to the household of Tavia, and I pray that she may be firmly rooted in faith and love, both carnal and spiritual. Give my regards to Alce, that most dear friend of mine, and to the incomparable Daphnus, and to Eutecnus, and to all the rest by name. Farewell in the grace of God!

IGNATIUS TO POLYCARP

Ignatius, also called Theophorus, sends heartiest greetings to Polycarp, who is bishop of the Church of Smyrna, or rather has for his bishop[1] God the Father and the Lord Jesus Christ.

1. I am so well pleased with your God-mindedness,[2] firmly built, as it were, upon an immovable rock, that I am exceedingly grateful for the privilege I had of seeing your saintly face. May it, please God, be a constant joy to me! 2 I exhort you, clothed as you are with the garment of grace, to speed on your course[3] and exhort all others to attend to their salvation. Do justice to your office[4] with the utmost solicitude, both physical and spiritual. Be concerned about unity, the greatest blessing. Bear with all,[5] just as the Lord does with you. *Have patience with all in charity,* as indeed you do. 3 To prayer give yourself unceasingly; beg for an increase in understanding; watch without letting your spirit flag. Speak to each one singly[6] in imitation of God's way. Bear the infirmities of all,[7] like a master athlete.[8] The greater the toil, the greater the reward.

2. If you love good disciples, you can expect no thanks.[9] Rather, reduce to subjection, by gentleness, the more pestiferous. Not every hurt is healed by the same plaster. Allay fits of fever by means of poultices. 2 *Be wary like a serpent, yet always guileless like a dove.*[10] You consist of body and soul for the reason that you may deal graciously with whatever meets your eye; but pray that what is kept secret may be revealed to you. In this way you will be lacking in nothing and abound in every gift. 3 As a pilot calls on winds and a storm-tossed mariner looks havenward, so the times call on you to win your way to God.[11] As God's athlete, be sober; the stake is immortality and eternal life. Of this you are firmly convinced. For your sake I sacrifice myself—chains and all, which are your delight.

3. Men that seem worthy of confidence, yet teach strange doctrines,[12] must not upset you. Stand firm, like an anvil under the hammer. It is like a great athlete to take blows and yet win the fight. For God's sake above all we must endure everything, so that God, in turn, may endure us. 2 Increase your zeal. Read the signs of the times. Look for Him who is above all time—the Timeless, the Invisible, who for our sake became visible, the Impassible, who became subject to suffering on our account and for our sake endured everything.

4. Widows must not be neglected.[13] After the Lord, you must be their guardian. Nothing must be done without your approval; nor must you do anything without God's approval, as indeed you do not. Be calm. 2 Let meetings be held as frequently as possible. Seek out all by name. 3 Do not treat slaves, male or female, with a haughty air, but neither must they give themselves airs; on the contrary, for the glory of God they should render all the better service so as to obtain a better freedom from God. They should not pine for release at the expense of the community; otherwise, they turn out to be slaves of unruly appetites.

5. Pay no attention to their wily stratagems;[14] and do more preaching on this subject. Tell my sisters to love the Lord and to be content with their husbands in body and soul.[15] In like manner, exhort my brethren in the name of Jesus Christ *to love their wives as the Lord loves the Church.*[16] 2 If anyone is able to remain continent, to the honor of the Flesh of the Lord, let him persistently avoid boasting.[17] The moment he boasts, he is lost; and if he is more highly esteemed than the bishop,[18] he is undone. For those of both sexes who contemplate marriage it is proper to enter the union with the sanction of the bishop; thus their marriage will be acceptable to the Lord and not just gratify lust. Let all things be done to the honor of God.

6. Heed the bishop, that God may heed you, too. My life is a ransom for those who are obedient to the bishop, presbyters, and deacons; and in their company may I obtain my portion! Toil together, wrestle together, run together, suffer together, rest together, rise together, since you are stewards in God's house, members of His household, and His servants.[19] 2 Win the approval of Him whose soldiers you are, from whom you also draw your pay. Let none of you turn deserter.[20] Let your baptism be your armor; your faith, your helmet; your love, your spear; your patient endurance, your panoply. Your deposits[21] should be your works, that you may receive your savings to the exact amount. To sum up: be long-suffering toward one another and gentle, as God is with you. May you be my joy always!

7. Since, as I was informed, the Church at Antioch in Syria enjoys peace through your prayer, I, too, gather fresh courage, carefree and confident in God. If only I win my way to God, for at the resurrection I want to be found your disciple! 2 It is fitting, my dear God-blessed Polycarp, to convene a council invested with all the splendor of God and to appoint someone who is dear to you and untiring in his

zeal, one qualified for the part of God's courier; then confer
on him the distinction of going to Syria and extolling, for the
glory of God, the untiring charity of your community. 3 A
Christian is not his own master; his time belongs to God.
This is God's work; and it will be yours, too, once you have
accomplished it. Yes, I trust in the grace of God that you are
ready for a noble work which concerns God. Knowing your
intense zeal for the truth, I confine my exhortation to these
few words.

8.   To conclude. Because of my sudden embarkation
from Troas for Neapolis—for such is the order of the day [22]—
I cannot personally write to all the Churches. Therefore,
God-minded as you are, you will please write to the principal
Churches [23] and tell them to do the same thing: those that
can afford it should send messengers; the rest should send
letters through the kindness of your personal delegates. You
are qualified for this task. In this way you all will reap honor
from a work destined to live forever. 2 Remember me to all
by name, especially to the widow [24] of Epitropus, with her
whole family and those of her children. Remember me to my
dear Attalus. Remember me to the man who will have the
honor of going to Syria. God's grace will forever be with
him, as also with Polycarp who sends him. 3 I say good-bye
to you all forever in Jesus Christ our God, through whom I
wish you to be united with God and under His watchful eye.
My greetings to Alice, that most dear friend of mine.
Farewell in the Lord!

NOTES

CLEMENT OF ROME

Introduction

[1] The term came into use when in 1686 J. B. Cotelier published a volume entitled, *Patres aevi apostolici*. It included Barnabas, Clement of Rome, Ignatius of Antioch, Hermas, and Polycarp of Smyrna. Later it became customary to add to these the *Didache*, the *Epistle to Diognetus*, Papias of Hierapolis, and Quadratus. It has been proposed in recent years to abandon this collective name so well established by usage. Questions of authorship and chronology raised by modern scholarship urge this. There is, however, a golden thread running through all these works that marks them out as a group by themselves—their Apostolic inspiration. They are, therefore, a welcome bridge between the New Testament and the post-canonical primitive Christian literature that follows. Removed from the Hellenistic philosophy and rhetoric of the time, they are a spontaneous flowering of the Holy Scriptures, and for a long time furnished in good part the customary reading at liturgical gatherings.

[2] See O. Bardenhewer, *Geschichte der altkirchlichen Literatur* I (2d ed., Freiburg i. Br. 1913) 119-22.

[3] *Ibid.*, 122.

THE EPISTLE TO THE CORINTHIANS

[1] This title is, of course, a later addition. The numeral letter " A " (— " First "), appearing in the chief manuscripts, was added by copyists to distinguish this epistle from the so-called " Second " Epistle of Clement, to which it was joined. See the Introduction, p. 4.

[2] The Gr. word rendered " to live (reside) as a stranger (alien, exile) " is so used in Luke 24. 18 and Heb. 11. 9. The verb and the corresponding noun emphasize transitoriness and non-citizenship. Cf. 1 Peter 2. 11: " I exhort you to be like strangers and exiles "; Phil. 3. 20: " Our true home is in heaven." For the same thought,

see 1 Peter 1. 1 and 17, and Heb. 11. 13. This detachment from the native soil or the world was one of the most strongly marked features of the Christian religion. The true hopes of a Christian are anchored, not in this world, but in the next. 1 Cor. 7. 31: "The visible form of this world is passing away" (F. A. Spencer). It was this otherworldliness that contributed so largely, as we know from the Ignatian letters, to the Christian's readiness to sacrifice this life that he might win the eternal. See Matt. 10. 39.

⁸ 1 Cor. 1. 2; Rom. 1. 7. Cf. Rom. 1. 6; 1 Cor. 1. 24; Rom. 8. 28, and compare Matt. 22. 14. The predicates "called" and "sanctified" recall St. Paul's frequent use of them to designate a "Christian." Clement wrote toward the close of the first century; yet, he is astonishingly familiar with the whole New Testament, which proves the rapidity with which the canonical writings spread over the whole Roman empire.

⁴ This terse expression of Christ's mediatorship (1 Tim. 2. 5) eventually found its way into the Roman liturgy, where every collect ends with the words: *per Christum Dominum nostrum.* Cf. A. Jungmann, *Die Stellung Christi im liturgischen Gebet* (Münster i. W. 1925).

⁵ This is the first instance of Clement's fondness for synonyms. An educated Roman would naturally be familiar with this means of emphasis. Nor is this the only indication of Clement's acquaintance with the ancient rhetorical theory. See note 106. The "calamities" were incidental to the persecution which the Roman Christians endured under Domitian. This epistle was "probably written towards the close of Domitian's reign or on the accession of Nerva" (Lightfoot).

⁶ The Corinthian schism came to the ears of the Roman Christians (see 47. 7), and Rome took action. See the Introduction, p. 4 f.

⁷ The adjective ἐπιεικής occurs frequently in the N. T.: cf. Phil. 4. 5; 1 Tim. 3. 3; Titus 3. 2; James 3. 17; 1 Peter 2. 18. Good English equivalents are: reasonable, fair, gentle, forbearing, thoughtful, considerate, courteous. In Phil. 4. 5 the Vulgate renders *modestia vestra.* "Note here and in the following the practical, ethical, and altogether unmystical character of Clement's Christianity" (Knopf). See notes 12, 15, 91, 95.

⁸ The noun γνῶσις is a favorite with St. Paul (23 instances) and is also used by St. Peter (4 instances). It was destined later to play an important part in combating the heresy known as Gnosticism.

See K. Bihlmeyer, *Kirchengeschichte* 1 (10th ed., Paderborn 1936), section 29.

⁹ Cf. Eph. 5. 21-24; Phil. 4. 8 f.; Col. 3. 18-21; Titus 2. 4 f.

¹⁰ Acts 20. 35.

¹¹ More than for earthly goods, the Corinthians cared for the spiritual sustenance furnished by Christ. The word ἐφόδιον (Lat. *viaticum*) signifies supplies for travelling, travelling allowance, means and ways, maintenance needed for life's pilgrimage.

¹² Acts 2. 17; Rom. 5. 5. Knopf takes offence at Clement's "rational moralism," which considers the outpouring of the Spirit as a *reward* of personal piety, "in contrast with St. Paul and St. John." But while God is free in bestowing His gifts, is it wrong or un-Christian to suppose that He may be more lavish in showering them on a fervent community than on one that does not strive to excel in the practice of virtue? See notes 7, 15, 91, 95.

¹³ The word ἀδελφότης occurs in 1 Peter 2. 7 and 5. 9. All Christians the wide world over are "brothers in Christ." For "the full number of His elect," see note 165.

¹⁴ Titus 3. 1; 2 Tim. 2. 21; 3. 17; 2 Cor. 9. 8.

¹⁵ Prov. 7. 3. "Note again Clement's moralism" (Knopf). See notes 7, 12, 91, 95.

¹⁶ Deut. 32. 15.

¹⁷ Isa. 3. 5.

¹⁸ Wisd. 2. 24.

¹⁹ Quoted from the Septuagint, Gen. 4. 3-8; but there are some divergences from the Hebrew text. In this epistle the same applies to other quotations from the Old Testament.

²⁰ Cain's sacrifice, it seems, was correct in form ("you offered rightly"), but was either marred by selfish motives or by reserving to himself the best, while giving God the worst (Lightfoot). See the commentators on Genesis. The next sentence is very obscure, since the reference of the pronoun αὐτοῦ is not clear.

²¹ Gen. 27. 41; 37.

²² Exod. 2. 14.

²³ Num. 12 and 16.

²⁴ 1 Kings 18.

²⁵ The word rendered "athlete" means, of course, combatant, fighter, champion. Metaphors from the Greek games are common in St. Paul and the early patristic writers. See, for instance, Ignatius, *Pol.* 1. 3; 2. 3; 3. 1. The expression "nearest to us (in time or in place)" is vague and is not much improved by the addition of "our

own generation." It seems evident, however, that Clement refers to the Neronian persecution. This epistle probably was written about 96.

²⁶ The word στῦλος is applied to St. Peter and other Apostles in Gal. 2. 9. They were "the main support" of the early Church.

²⁷ The word μαρτυρεῖν came early to be used for "sealing one's testimony with blood." Cf. Acts 22. 20; 1 Tim. 6. 13. It is not always possible to decide which sense prevails, "to give testimony" or "to die as a martyr for the faith." See Lightfoot's note; also H. Delehaye, "Martyr et confesseur," Anal. Bolland. 39 (1921) 20-49, and H. v. Campenhausen, Die Idee des Martyriums in der alten Kirche (Göttingen 1936); also, E. Peterson, Zeuge der Wahrheit (Leipzig 1937).

²⁸ See Acts 9. 25, 30; 13. 50; 14. 6; 17. 10, 14; 20. 3; 2 Cor. 11. 25, 33.

²⁹ Literally, "the extremity of the West." In Rom. 15. 24 St. Paul speaks of his intention of visiting Spain. Cf. E. Barnikol, Spanienreise und Römerbrief (Halle 1934).

³⁰ Tacitus (Ann. 15. 44) speaks of a multitudo ingens.

³¹ The reference is of course to Rome.

³² The "Danaids and Dircae" are evidently Christian women who were subjected to tortures not unlike those inflicted on the daughters of Danaus and on Dirce who were known to the readers from Greek mythology. Dirce was tied to the horns of a bull and thus dragged to death. The Danaids were slain, but their special manner of death is not known. For ancient literary references to these women, see the notes on this passage by Lightfoot and Knopf. Compare Tertullian, Apol. 15, and Martial, Epigrams 7, 8, 16, and 21.

³³ Gen. 2. 23. The "mighty cities" and "powerful nations" would naturally include Troy, Babylon, Carthage, Numantia, Corinth, and, above all, Jerusalem.

³⁴ Cf. 1 Peter 1. 19.

³⁵ Wisd. 12, 10. On the concept of μετάνοια (occurring 8 times in this chapter and the next) as "change of heart," "conversion," etc., see A. H. Dirksen, The New Testament Concept of Metanoia (diss. Catholic University of America: Washington 1932); H. Pohlmann, Die Metanoia als Zentralbegriff der christlichen Frömmigkeit. Eine kritische und systematische Untersuchung zum ordo salutis auf biblisch-theologischer Grundlage (Leipzig 1938). Note that in about 20 passages in this epistle Clement speaks of God as "the Master," a designation not common in modern speech. The idea is

the same that prompted St. Paul to call himself the δοῦλος or " slave "
of Christ.

³⁶ Gen. 7.

³⁶ᵃ Jonas 3; Matt. 12. 41.

³⁷ Literally, " they were strangers to God," not being members of
the Chosen People.

³⁸ Ezech. 33. 11-27.

³⁹ Isa. 1. 16-20.

⁴⁰ The sense seems to be: " If you do these things, I give you the
right to complain in case I do not answer your prayers."

⁴¹ Gen. 5. 24; Heb. 11. 5.

⁴² Gen. 6. 8 ff.; 7. 1; Heb. 11. 7; 2 Peter 2. 5.

⁴³ Isa. 41. 8; 2 Par. 20. 7; James 2. 23.

⁴⁴ Gen. 12. 1-3.

⁴⁵ Gen. 13. 14-16.

⁴⁶ Gen. 15. 5, 6; Rom. 4. 3. On this extremely important text, see
the standard biblical and theological treatises. The literal meaning
is clear: Abraham believed God who had said that He would make
him the father of a numerous posterity; " and it (this belief in the
truth of God's word) was reckoned (accepted) in his favor as justification." In biblical Greek εἰς with the accusative often replaces the
predicate nominative. See below, 31. 2, and 32. 4.

⁴⁷ Gen. 21. 22; Heb. 11. 17.

⁴⁸ Gen. 19; 2 Peter 2. 6, 7.

⁴⁹ Jos. 2; James 2. 25; Heb. 11. 31.

⁵⁰ Jos. 2; see the entire chapter.

⁵¹ Jer. 9. 23 f.; 1 Kings 2. 10; 1 Cor. 1. 31; 2 Cor. 10. 17.

⁵² Matt. 5. 7; 6. 14, 15; 7. 1, 2, 12; Luke 6. 31, 36-38.

⁵³ Isa. 66. 2.

⁵⁴ Prov. 2. 21, 22; Ps. 36. 9, 38.

⁵⁵ Ps. 36. 35-37.

⁵⁶ Isa. 29. 13; Mark 7. 6.

⁵⁷ Ps. 61. 5; 77. 36, 37; 30. 19; 11. 4-6.

⁵⁸ Isa. 53. 1-12.

⁵⁹ Ps. 21. 7-9.

⁶⁰ Heb. 11. 37.

⁶¹ Isa. 41. 8; 2 Par. 20. 7; James 2. 23; Gen. 18. 27.

⁶² Job. 1. 1; 14. 4, 5.

⁶³ Num. 12. 7; Heb. 3. 2, 5; Exod. 3. 11; 4. 10. The source of the
second quotation is unknown. The use of καπνός, etc., for worthless

things and, especially, the perishableness of life, was known to the ancients; Knopf quotes Empedocles, Seneca, and Marcus Aurelius.

[64] Ps. 88. 21; 1 Kings 13. 14; Acts 13. 22.

[65] Ps. 50. 3-19.

[66] To achieve "peace" in the sadly distracted Corinthian community, Clement points out that God's blessings are conditioned on men's humility, modesty, and obedience. This is the great lesson most needed by the Corinthians at the present moment. He then passes on to a magnificent eulogy of the cosmos and its orderly arrangement or administration (διοίκησις). The "goal" to be reached in our daily lives is none other than that "goal of peace handed down to us from the beginning," when God created heaven and earth and laid the foundations of peace and harmony in the world. For the word λόγια, see note 179. A μεμαρτυρημένος is one "on whom favorable judgment has been passed"; or, in this context, one "on whom testimonials so eulogistic have been showered" (J. Donovan, *The Logia in Ancient and Recent Literature* (Cambridge 1924) 16.

[67] Heb. 12. 1.

[68] The following exposition is a picture on a grand scale of the orderliness that characterizes the physical world. It was Clement's idea, as it was that of the contemporary Stoics, that a man's private life should reflect the order so visible in the macrocosm; and since the cosmos according to the Stoics was divine, it was only through this harmony with it that man could partake of the divine. This is the meaning of their well-known principle of morality expressed in the maxim: *secundum naturam vivere*. But if Clement's language is strongly tinged with Stoic ideas current at the time, especially at Rome, yet the gulf between Stoicism and Christianity is sharply brought out by his belief and statement that God is a personal Being that *created* the world. For expressions of Stoic admiration for the cosmos, we may compare Cicero's De natura deorum, 2. 47-57; 98-104, and his *Somnium Scipionis* 15. Seneca, too, affords many parallels; see *Ad Marciam* 18; *Ad Helviam* 8; *Natur. quaest.* 5. 13 ff.; De benefic. 4. 25.

In general, it must be remembered that the Fathers depended for their knowledge of the cosmos primarily on the Bible (Genesis, the Book of Job, the Psalms). At the same time, they had no scruple in availing themselves of the ready-made Stoic vocabulary when terms were wanted to express their ideas. An instance in point is the use of the term δημιουργός for "Creator," stripped, of course, of its pagan connotations. To them, as to the Stoics, God was πατήρ and εὐεργέτης.

Both believed in God's διοίκησις (arrangement, administration) of the world, though each in his own way. Cf. G. Bardy, "Expressions stoiciennes dans la Prima Clementis," *Rech. des sciences rel.* 12 (1922) 73-85. In this connection, E. H. Blakeney, *The Hymn of Cleanthes* (London 1921) may be read with profit.

69 Job 38. 11.

70 The "boundless sea" is probably the Mediterranean; the "ocean" mentioned later is assumed to be the Atlantic. The expression, "the stations of the winds" (10), seems to imply that each of the four prevailing winds has, as it were, its regular station or quarter, from which it blows at its proper time.

71 After the precedent set by St. Paul (as in Rom. 1. 25) of interrupting the narrative or the exposition by a doxology, such sudden praises of God are common in the Fathers. In Clement it occurs again in 32. 4; 38. 4; 43. 6; 45. 7; 50. 7; 58. 2; 61. 3; 64.

72 Prov. 20. 27.

73 Heb. 4. 12.

74 Ps. 33. 12-18; 31. 10.

75 The source of this quotation is unknown.

76 Isa. 14. 1; Mal. 3. 1.

77 1 Cor. 15. 20 ff.

78 1 Cor. 15. 35-38; Matt. 13. 3.

79 The myth of the phoenix was well known in antiquity since Hesiod and Herodotus. Ovid tells the story in *Metam.* 15. 392-407. Another reference to it is in Pliny the Elder, *Hist. Nat.* 10. 2; again, in Tacitus, *Ann.* 6. 34. Mention of the bird is also found in Jewish authors. Clement seems to have been the first Christian writer to make use of the myth, which became quite popular after him, as is also attested by early Christian art. Perhaps the best-known account in Christian literature is that of a poem attributed to Lactantius (for text, commentary, and translation, cf. M. C. FitzPatrick, *De ave Phoenice* [diss. University of Pennsylvania: Philadelphia 1933]).

80 The source of this quotation is unknown; but see Ps. 27. 7 and 87. 11. The Gr. word ἐξομολογεῖν (or the middle), in Latin generally rendered *confiteri*, means "to confess freely (openly, publicly)," as in Mark 1. 5, or "to profess (acknowledge) openly and joyfully," as here, or "to promise, "engage," "agree," as in Luke 22. 6.

81 Job 19. 26—freely quoted.

82 Heb. 10. 23; 11. 11; Ps. 144. 14.—Heb. 6. 18.

83 Wisd. 9. 1; Heb. 1. 3; Wisd. 12. 12; 11. 22.

84 Ps. 18. 2-4.

[85] Ps. 138. 7-10.

[86] Deut. 32. 8, 9.

[87] Deut. 4. 34; Num. 18. 27; 2 Par. 31. 14; Ezech. 48. 12; Deut. 14. 2.

[88] Prov. 3. 34; James 4. 6; Peter 5. 5.

[89] Job 11. 2, 3.

[90] Rom. 2. 29.

[91] Gen. 12. 2, 3; 18. 18; Gal. 3. 14; James 2. 21 ff. (Abraham), Gen. 22. 7 ff. (Isaac), Gen. 28 f. (Jacob). For the expression "enabled by faith," see Gal. 3.14; others take the preposition διά in a weaker sense, as in Rom. 2. 27. The sense of the phrase "*because* he knew the future" is not clear, since the Scripture does not say that he foresaw the Sacrifice of Christ. The Greek may, however, mean: "*although* he knew what was in store for him." Knopf is irritated by Clement's uttering πίστις (faith) and ποιεῖν (to do) in the same breath. See above notes 7, 12, 15; also 95, and 146.

[92] Rom. 9. 4, 5.

[93] Gen. 15. 5; 22. 17; 26. 4.

[94] Rom. 3. 28.

[95] See Rom. 6. 1. After explaining that Abraham was justified by faith" (ch. 4) and that this faith comes "through Jesus Christ" (ch. 5), St. Paul insists that it does not follow that therefore we may "continue in sin." Clement argues similarly: "Shall we rest from *doing good* and give up *love?*" Knopf takes this occasion to contrast the Apostle's "Solafidismus" with Clement's "Synergismus"; with what right, the reader may judge for himself. Knopf forgets that the "mystic" St. Paul was at the same time the greatest Christian "moralizer."

[96] Titus 3. 1; 2 Tim. 2. 21; 3. 17; 2 Cor. 9. 8.

[97] Gen. 1. 26, 27.

[98] Gen. 1. 28, 22.

[99] Isa. 40. 10; 62. 11; Prov. 24. 12; Ps. 61. 13.

[100] Titus 3. 1.

[101] Dan. 7. 10; Isa. 6. 3. See also Apoc. 4. 8. The passage in Clement is sometimes regarded as the earliest indication of the use of the Sanctus (*tersanctus, trisagium*) in the liturgy of primitive Christianity; cf. H. Engberding, "Trishagion," *Lex. für Theol. und Kirche* 10 (1938) 295. For ready reference see also H. T. Henry, "Agios O Theos," *Cath. Encyclopedia* 1 (1907) 211 f., and A. Fortescue, "Sanctus," *ibid.* 13 (1912) 432-4.

[102] Acts 2. 1.

[103] 1 Cor. 2. 9; cf. Isa. 64. 4; 65. 16. Note, in the following, 35. 2, Clement's magnificent summing up of "the gifts of God" which we enjoy as Christians: life, sanctifying grace, which is the pledge of immortality; joyousness, which is not marred by, but coexists with, and is born of, the keeping of the commandments; truth, the true knowledge of God, which empowers us to speak to Him without fear, being His children; faith, so certain that it begets absolute trust and confidence; continence, chastity, self-mastery, without which there is no holiness. The preposition "with" here represents the Gr. ἐν, denoting that in each pair the second item is "involved (included, embedded) in" the first, or that the first is essentially connected with the second. For another equally magnificent summation, see 36. 2 and note 106.

[104] Rom. 1. 29-32.

[105] Ps. 49. 16-23.

[106] Heb. 2. 17, 18; 3. 1; 4. 15. Note this summing up (see note 103) of the glories of our High Priest Jesus Christ, which has no equal in early literature for splendor of expression or depth of thought. Each of the following four sentences begins with διὰ τούτου, "through Him," or, more literally, "He it is through whom"—a device well known to the ancient rhetoricians.

[107] Cf. 2 Cor. 3. 18.

[108] Heb. 1. 3, 4.

[109] Ps. 103. 4; Heb. 1. 7.—Ps. 2. 7, 8; Heb. 1. 5.

[110] Ps. 109. 1; Heb. 1. 13.

[111] 1 Cor. 15. 23.

[112] For the following cf. 1 Cor. 12. 12 ff.; 12. 21, 22.

[113] "The whole of our body"; a reference, evidently, to the whole Church, which is one body in Christ—the Mystical Body. This subject, always a favorite one with the Fathers, has evoked numerous studies in recent decades; the bibliography has been collected by J. Bluett: "The Mystical Body of Christ: 1890-1940," *Theol. Studies* 3 (1942) 260-89. The modern consciousness of this most intimate union of Christ and the Church has been authoritatively voiced in the encyclical letter given to the world by the present Pope, Pius XII, in 1943: *Mystici Corporis.* See note 137, 143, and 146. Paragraphs 1 and 2 of this chapter show that the "Social Question" was a burning problem even in Clement's time, and it is significant that he finds its solution in his conception of the Mystical Body. Cf. I. Giordani, *Il messagio sociale dei primi Padri della Chiesa* (Turin

1938; also trans. into English by A. I. Zizzamia [Paterson 1944])
passim.

[114] Rom. 12. 4 ff.; 1 Cor. 16. 17; Phil. 2. 30.

[115] In 1 Cor. 16. 17 and Phil. 2.30, the word ὑστέρημα is used in a different sense.

[116] Literally, "the one who is holy in the flesh."

[117] Job 4. 16-18; 15. 15; 4. 19-5. 5.

[118] Rom. 11. 33 (R. Knox: "the mine of God's knowledge"); 1 Cor. 2. 10.

[119] Clement is proving his point by an illustration from the Old Testament as though the temple and its services were still existing. As the Apostolic Fathers speak of bishop, presbyters, and deacons, so Clement here adopts the Jewish terminology (high priest, priests, and Levites) in the same sense. See note 125.

[120] This is the first instance in Christian literature of the use of λαϊκός, "layman." To express the notion of "the laity" Ignatius coined the phrase οἱ κατ' ἄνδρα; see Ignatius, *Ephes.* notes 15 and 48.

[121] 1 Cor. 15. 23.

[122] In the New Testament ναός is the name for the holy place, the Sanctuary, in front of which stood the altar. For the Jewish sacrifices, see Exod. 29. 38-42; Num. 28. 3-8; 6. 13 ff.; Lev. 4. 3 ff.; 14. 13-17, 24-28.

[123] Clement uses ἀπό (not ἐκ, for which see, for example, John 8. 23): "with a message from." Cf. Luke 1. 26.

[124] Titus 1. 5; Rom. 16. 5. For Clement there is only one way of holding legitimate authority in the Church: it originates with God, is communicated through Christ to the Apostles, and from these is passed on to their legitimate successors. Only a decade or so later, Ignatius, bishop of Antioch, makes this "Apostolic succession" the starting point of almost all his exhortations addressed to the Churches in Asia.

[125] Isa. 60. 17. In Clement the terms ἐπίσκοπος and πρεσβύτερος are still synonymous. Compare 21. 6; 44. 5; 47. 6; 54. 2; 57. 1. The "bishops" in Isaias are, of course, overseers, superintendents, magistrates. See note 129.

[126] Num. 12. 7; Heb. 3. 2, 5.

[127] Num. 17.

[128] Cf. John 17. 3.

[129] It is not always clear from the context whether Clement uses the words ἐπίσκοπος and ἐπισκοπή in the sense of "bishop" and "episcopate." See note 125. The word δῶρα, as proper to the

"episcopate," seems to include sacrifices, alms, prayers, contributions to the agape, and the Eucharist. Each official is supposed to offer the δῶρα that belong to his sacred ministry (λειτουργία).

¹⁸⁰ The word τόπος admits of two interpretations. Either: "these men will not be dislodged from the *place* which has been built for them," that is, heaven (cf. Matt. 25. 34); or: "being dead, they are no longer exposed to the danger of ejection from their *office*." For the former sense, see Clem. 5. 4 and 7.

¹⁸¹ Here, again, two interpretations are possible; the one, given in the text, harmonizes with the whole tone and purpose of this epistle; the other: "Contend zealously, if you will, but let your zeal be directed to things pertaining to salvation" (Lightfoot). In the latter case, we have to read ἔστε (the imperative).

¹³² Since many "unjust and fraudulent things" *are* written in the Scriptures, γέγραπται must obviously be given a fuller sense: "written and approved as a precedent for future conduct." When the Fathers introduce a text with the word γέγραπται, they mean to quote it as having the *authority and approval* of Holy Scripture. Hence here, negatively: there is no scriptural authority or approval for unjust and fraudulent actions; there would be such authority if good men were instanced as having been repudiated by holy men.

¹³³ Dan. 6. 16, 17; 3. 19 ff.

¹³⁴ The source of the first quotation is uncertain. For the second, see Ps. 17. 26, 27, where "Thou" refers to God: He deals with men according to their character. Clement here accommodates the words of the Psalmist to another sense. The words of Holy Scripture are so sacred, so meaningful, and couched in such pregnant language, that they were often applied in a so-called accommodated sense. This use runs through the writings of the Fathers and the liturgy of the Church. See Romans 15. 4.

¹³⁵ James 4. 1.

¹³⁶ Eph. 4. 4-6.

¹³⁷ "We are members of one another"; Rom. 12. 5. The translation in the text is that of F. A. Spencer. In the following, 37. 4 and 46. 5-7, there is clear proof that Clement was acquainted with the doctrine of the Mystical Body of Christ. See note 113.

¹³⁸ Matt. 26. 24; Luke 17. 1, 2; Mark 9. 42.

¹³⁹ Phil. 4. 15 (="soon after your conversion to Christianity").

¹⁴⁰ 1 Cor. 1. 10 ff.

¹⁴¹ We are accustomed to speak of Christian education, etc.; how

much richer and more meaningful is Clement's expression, "your training *in* Christ"! See notes 113 and 143.

[142] Clement, evidently, was not appealed to by the Corinthians for a decision in their dispute, but wrote to them, as it were, *motu proprio*. "The people differing from us in religion" are the Jews and the pagans. A proper regard for the respect of "outsiders" is inculcated frequently from the very beginning of Christianity; see, for example, Matt. 5. 16; 1 Cor. 10. 32 ("Give no offence to either Jew or Greek"); 1 Thess. 4. 12; 1 Tim. 6. 1; 1 Peter 2. 15; also Ignatius, *Trall.* 8. 2.

[143] Ps. 117. 19, 20. Note that in § 4 the preposition "of" in "observance *of* the law" and "the gate *of* Christ" is a poor substitute for the more vigorous use of *ἐν* in the original. St. Paul's use of "in Christ" was widely copied by the early Fathers as a reminder of his teaching that the Church is the "body of Christ." Cf. his epistle to the Ephesians. See notes 113 and 146.

[144] Luke 1. 75.

[145] A reference to the *charismata* which were so plentifully bestowed upon the Corinthians; see above, 13. 1 and 38. 1 f. The rebellious members of the Corinthian community seem to have possessed, or boasted of possessing, all the "graces" mentioned in this paragraph. In the value Clement sets upon these extraordinary phenomena, he is at one with St. Paul (1 Cor. 13. 13): "he (the person so blessed) must seek the common good and not his personal advantage." The "wise" or "skilled" man here referred to is one who knows how to discern what is right or wrong in the discourses made by others. The word rendered "pure" generally implies sexual purity or virginity. See note 116. The "continent" are often warned not to boast of their gift; see 38. 2.

[146] The "love in Christ": the love founded in Christ and establishing that intimate "union with Christ" explained in John 15. See also John 14. 15; 1 John 5. 1-3, and note 113. It is noteworthy that both Clement and Ignatius insist again and again upon the need of "love" in addition to that of "faith." See notes 91 and 95.

[147] Col. 3. 14.

[148] Prov. 10. 12; 1 Peter 4. 8; James 5. 20; esp. 1 Cor. 13. 4-7; 1 John 2. 5; 4. 17 ff. Note Clement's beautiful variation of St. Paul's encomium of love. With him the "love of God" is now God's love for us, and now our love for God. Love both giving and receiving—this is true Christian mysticism. It will not do to play off "the

mysticism of Paul and John" (Knopf) against that of Clement, the
matter-of-fact Roman. See note 7.

[149] Isa. 26. 20. Clement says that the souls of the pious before
Christ's coming (when God's anger lay upon the world) were kept,
barred from heaven, in a separate place or prison (the *Limbo
Patrum*) until Christ after His Resurrection released them.

[150] Ps. 31. 1, 2; Rom. 4. 7-9.

[151] Num. 16; Ps. 48. 15. Here the new Latin Psalter, published
by the Pontifical Biblical Institute in 1945, reads: Infernus erit
domus eorum.

[152] Exod. 14.

[153] Ps. 68. 31-33.

[154] Ps. 49. 14, 15; 50. 19.

[155] Exod. 34. 28; Deut. 9. 9; for the following, see Deut. 9. 12;
9. 13, 14; Exod. 32. 31, 32. "I will make you the ruler of a mighty
nation": this is, evidently, the sense of the underlying Semitic
expression: "I will *make you into* a mighty nation."

[156] It has been surmised that the sentiment here expressed
prompted Clement, who was ordained by St. Peter, to make room for
Linus as the Apostle's immediate successor in the episcopacy.

[157] Ps. 23. 1. In the new Psalter (see note 151) this verse reads:
Domini est terra et quae replent eam. In the following sentence the
Gr. word for "living *as citizens*" should be given full weight. It
recalls Phil. 3. 20.

[158] The reference here is either to the Roman Christians or to
Christians in general. Later in the history of the Church the
ransom of Christian captives became an established practice.

[159] Judith 8 ff.

[160] Esth. 4. 16.

[161] Ps. 117. 18: *Castigavit, castigavit me Dominus.* For the following citations cf. Prov. 3. 12; Heb. 12. 6; Ps. 140. 5; Job 5. 17-26.

[162] 1 Peter 5. 5. "Submit to the presbyters": the exact words
which St. Peter, the first bishop of Rome, made use of. Note the
stern tone adopted by his successor. Is this a mere matter of chance?
See the Introduction, p. 4, and note 164.

Submissiveness to duly established ecclesiastical authority is an
ever-recurring theme in the Apostolic Fathers, in whose writings the
verb ὑποτάσσεσθαι, rendered "submit," and its cognates are used 26
times. The verb rendered "accept correction" often shades over into
"submit to disciplining and chastisement." See Luke 23. 16. The
expression "the flock of Christ" recalls Luke 12. 32.

[163] Prov. 1. 23-33. In ecclesiastical usage the word *Wisdom* is a collective title for the Book of Wisdom, Proverbs, Ecclesiasticus, and Ecclesiastes.

[164] "By Him through us": Clement speaks as though he were conscious of being more than just the bishop of another diocese. See note 162.

[165] Clement speaks of a well-fixed, well-determined (lit., "recounted in detail"; "told exactly") number of the elect; but the epistle as a whole is proof that he was not what was later called a predestinarian.

The word παῖς may be taken strictly as "Son," or, in a wider sense, as "Servant" (see Matt. 12. 18). The scriptural reference following is from Acts 26. 18.

[166] Here Clement suddenly breaks into a solemn prayer addressed to God the Father. It extends from 59. 3 to 61. 4. It is one of the most precious gems preserved in early Christian literature. We should, perhaps, take for granted that Clement merely reproduces a prayer used Sunday after Sunday in the Roman liturgy. Examples of such a sudden outburst of religious emotion may be found in the Gospels, as in Matt. 12. 18-21 and in John 17. Cf. A. Baumstark, "Trisagion und Qedusha," *Jahrb. f. Liturgiewissenschaft* 3 (1923) 18-32; J. Marty, "Étude des textes cultuels de prière conservés par les 'Pères apostoliques,'" *Rev. d'hist. et de phil. rel.* 10 (1930) 90-95.

[167] Eph. 1. 18. In the following Clement draws upon Isa. 57. 15, 13. 11, Job 5. 11, 1 Kings 2. 7, Luke 1. 53, Deut. 32. 39, Num. 16. 22, 27. 16, Esth. 5. 1.

[168] Judith 9. 11.

[169] Ps. 118. 114; 78. 13; 94. 7; 99. 3.

[170] 1 Kings 8. 60; 2 Kings 19. 19; Ezech. 36. 23; Ps. 78. 13; 94. 7; 99. 3.

[171] Wisd. 7. 17; Ps. 88. 12, 13; 118. 137; 103. 1 ff.; 146. 5.

[172] Joel 2. 13; Eccli. 2. 11. For the following see Ps. 39. 3; 118. 133; Deut. 12. 25, 28; 13. 18; 21. 9. "Our rulers," that is, both temporal and ecclesiastical.

[173] Ps. 66. 2; 79. 4, 8, 20; Num. 6. 25, 26.

[174] Luke 1. 71; Ps. 105. 10; 17. 18; 37. 20.

[175] Ps. 144. 18; 146. 9; 1 Tim. 2. 7. The following part of the prayer (60. 4-61. 2) has been termed "a grand testimony" to the profound conviction of early Christianity, that the authority of the state and of state officials is from God (see Rom. 13. 1). This conviction was sublimated in the liturgical prayer of the Christian

communities, as here at Rome. Cf. F. J. Dölger, "Zur antiken und frühchristlichen Auffassung der Herrschergewalt von Gottes Gnaden," *Antike und Christentum* 3 (1932), esp. 118 f. Similar prayers for rulers are in use in the Church today. We pray for their welfare and bow to them, so, however, as not to "oppose the will of God." See also L. Biehl, *Das liturgische Gebet für Kaiser und Reich. Ein Beitrag zur Geschichte des Verhältnisses von Kirche u. Staat* (Paderborn 1937).

176 1 Tim. 17; Tob. 13. 6, 10.

177 Deut. 12. 25, 28; 13. 18.

178 Heb. 2. 17; 3. 1; 1 Peter 2. 25.

179 The word here rendered "the writings" deserves special attention. In 19. 1, it primarily refers to revelation, yet with implied connotation of Holy Writ. In 53. 1, the "oracles of God" are simply God's Word, His inspired Word, His revelation; and this is found in Holy Writ. The third reference to λόγια is in the present chapter. "God's educative oracles" or "God's oracular teaching" cannot otherwise be interpreted than as revelation viewed in its moral and educational effects. This sense of λόγια has been established by J. Donovan, *The Logia in Ancient and Recent Literature* (Cambridge 1924).

180 Eccli. 51. 34; Rom. 16. 4.

181 The Gr. word for "witnesses" contains an almost juridical connotation: "these men are to give reliable information to *us* of *your* conduct."

182 Num. 16. 22; 27. 16; Heb. 12. 9;–Deut. 14. 2; 26. 18; Exod 19. 5; Ps. 134. 4; Titus 2. 14.

183 Heb. 2. 17; 3. 1.

184 See note 1.

IGNATIUS OF ANTIOCH

INTRODUCTION

[1] Eduard Norden, a competent judge of ancient literature, regards Ignatius's letters as the most exquisite part of the literary remains of this time. See his *Die antike Kunstprosa* (Leipzig 1923) 2. 510.

[2] Note the accent on the word *Theophórus* (Θεοφόρος), "God-bearer"—not *Theóphorus* (Θεόφορος), "God-borne." That Ignatius's surname was actually pronounced to express the former meaning, is well argued by J. B. Lightfoot, *The Apostolic Fathers*, part 2: S. *Ignatius, S. Polycarp* (London 1889) 1. 25-28 and 2. 21-23. See also *Ephes.* note 27.

[3] A noble tribute to the character and the enlightened mind of Ignatius will be found in a eulogy preserved among a series of sermons preached on the Antiochian bishops by another illustrious son of Antioch, St. John Chrysostom. See *In S. Martyrem Ignatium* 1 (MG 50. 588).

[4] A good summary of the controversy in England is given by J. H. Srawley, *The Epistles of St. Ignatius* (Society for Promoting Christian Knowledge, London 1935) 9-20. See also O. Bardenhewer, *Geschichte der altkirchlichen Literatur* 1 (2nd ed., Freiburg i. Br. 1913) 143-50.

[5] See the excellent treatise by H. de Genouillac, *L'Église chrétienne au temps de saint Ignace d'Antioche* (Paris 1907).

[6] Read J. H. Newman, "The Theology of the Seven Epistles of St. Ignatius," *Essays Critical and Historical* 1 sect. 5 (London 1912).

[7] For the former, see, for example, L. Marchal, "Judéo-Chrétiens," *Dict. de théol. cath.* 8. 2 (1925) 1681-709; for the latter, G. Bareille, "Docétisme," *op. cit.*, 4. 2 (1910) 1484-501. Cf. also C. C. Richardson, *The Christianity of Ignatius of Antioch* (New York 1935) 51-54: "Heresy."

[8] See especially Norden, *op. cit.* 510-12.

TO THE EPHESIANS

Following the example of the greatest Christian letter writer, Ignatius opens his epistles with a studied greeting, only slightly varied by the circumstances of the community addressed. But what a difference! Compared with Ignatius, St. Paul seems chary of words and almost lacking in warmth of tone. The warm-hearted Ignatius, on the other hand, is rich and even exuberant in expression and generous in acknowledging all the virtues and prerogatives of his addressees. He certainly embraced Christianity with fervor and is anxious to let all the world know what a joy it is to be a Christian. Another point of difference between the epistles of these two men is that, while those of St. Paul are really doctrinal treatises in epistolary form, those of Ignatius approach more closely the ideal of familiar effusions. But a marked likeness between the two writers is the fact that " God the Father " and " the Lord Jesus Christ " were in the centre of their lives. Cf. H. Korn, *Die Nachwirkungen der Christus-mystik des Paulus in den apostolischen Vätern* (Leipzig 1928).

[1] The reference to Christ's " true " or " real suffering " is a first inkling of Ignatius's unremitting zeal in combating the dangerous heresy called Docetism, which denied the reality of Our Lord's human nature. See note 7 of the Introduction and the prefatory note to *Trall.*

[2] The Greek wording allows of another interpretation: the Ephesians owed their reputation to " a natural disposition, a constitutional trait, made right (δικαίᾳ)," or to " a temperament rectified (that is, supernaturalized) by faith and love through Jesus Christ." This tallies well with what follows: because they had been " restored to new life in the Blood of God " (that is, had become Christians), they were enabled to change their natural benevolence into the Christian virtue of charity. Note the preposition κατά, " conformably to."

[3] By way of background, the reader will do well to compare St. Paul's letter to the same Church, especially 1. 3-23. Both writers are familiar with the expression " imitators of God," used by the Apostle in 5. 1. See *Trall.* note 7. Cf. T. Preiss, " La mystique de l'imitation du Christ et de l'unité chez Ignace d'Antioche," *Rev. d'hist. et de phil. rel.* 18 (1938) 197-241.

[4] The idea of becoming a true " disciple " of Christ must have

9[1]

taken strong hold of Ignatius, and, no doubt, of the early Christians generally. For Ignatius to be a true disciple and to lay down his life for Christ was one and the same thing. This recalls several of Our Lord's utterances; as, for example, Luke 14. 26 and 27. See note 11. The possibility of martyrdom lay within the horizon of every ancient Christian. On the *Martyrergeist* of the early Christians, see K. Prümm, *Christentum als Neuheitserlebnis* (Freiburg i. Br. 1939) 348-57. The words "you hastened *to see me*" are an echo of Matt. 25. 36.

⁵ This seems to have been a different person from the slave of the same name whom St. Paul returned to his master Philemon.

⁶ Literally, "your bishop in the flesh." St. Paul's epistles are replete with instances of the various senses of the word σάρξ (flesh), especially when contrasted with πνεῦμα (Spirit). In the latter case, the precise meaning of the two expressions is not always obvious. Here the rendering "your bishop *here on earth*" does not exhaust the meaning of σάρξ; it seems to imply that Onesimus was their *visible* bishop, in contrast with their invisible bishop, Christ. Cf. 1 Peter 2. 25. See note 17, and *Pol.* note 1.

⁷ Such abrupt benedictions, or outbursts of praise and thanks to God, are common in the letters of St. Paul: Rom. 1. 25; 9. 5; 2 Cor. 1. 3; 11. 31; Eph. 1. 3; also 1 Peter 1. 3.

⁸ "This expression is with great propriety confined in Ignatius to *deacons*, since the function which the bishop had in common with them was *ministration; Magn.* 2; *Philad.* 4; *Smyrn.* 12" (Lightfoot). Note, however, that St. Paul, in calling Epaphras and Tychicus "fellow servants" or "fellow slaves" in Col. 1. 7 and 4. 7, seems to put these co-workers on a level with himself, both being "slaves" of Christ like himself (Phil. 1. 1).

⁹ Submissiveness to authority is one of the key notes in all Ignatius's exhortations to the several churches—a proof of the strictly monarchical constitution of the Church. The word rendered "sanctified" may also mean "consecrated," that is, to the service of God; or "dedicated," that is, to the truth, as in John 17. 19.

¹⁰ The expression "the Name" for "the name of Christ" is perhaps a reminiscence of St. Paul, Phil. 2. 9: "The name that is above any other name." A Christian, when speaking of "the Name," was understood to refer to Christ, which recalls the biblical use of "the name of God" for "the nature, essence, majesty of God." See above, 1. 2.

¹¹ For Ignatius's idea of "discipleship" see note 4. The noun

μαθητής and the verb μαθητεύειν have a distinctly Christian ring, which
is best expressed by "disciple" and "to initiate into discipleship."
Compare Our Lord's injunction in Matt. 28. 19: "Initiate all nations
in discipleship." The words "I am not yet perfected in Jesus Christ"
show Ignatius's terseness and virility of expression, since the Greek
word rendered "perfected" literally means—to use our modern educational parlance—"I am not yet *graduated* in (the school of) Jesus
Christ; I am right now only a *freshman* (ἀρχὴν ἔχω)." This recalls
the verb used in Luke 6. 40: "No disciple is above his teacher: even
when *fully trained*, that is, graduated, he is at best only like his
teacher," and, above, in 2. 2.

¹² Like St. Paul, Ignatius borrows metaphors from the great Greek
games, with which every reader was well acquainted. See, for
instance, 1 Cor. 9. 24 and Phil. 3. 14. See *Pol.* note 3.

¹³ The word rendered "inseparable" is used in several different
senses. See *Trall.* note 5. When Christ is called "the mind of the
Father," the word γνώμη includes the intellect as well as the will. See
Philad. note 3. For the connotations of St. John's λόγος, applied to
Christ by Ignatius in *Magn.* 8. 2, see the commentators.

¹⁴ The expression "the vast, wide earth" is intended to reproduce
the Greek τὰ πέρατα; literally, "the *farthest* parts (of the earth)."
Ignatius means, of course, the bishops appointed "the world over,
even including those at the farthest ends."

¹⁵ The Greek phrase rendered "the rank and file" deserves special
attention. A rendering like "individually," "severally," "man for
man" (for which see 20. 2 and note 48), does not always do justice
to it. Words in general receive their special color from the context;
so the word ἀνήρ may mean: man, grown-up man, husband, individual, person, soldier (as we speak of the *men* in the service), etc.,—
always in keeping with the context. In the present passage, as in
several others in these letters, the reference is to *men* or *persons* in
contrast with those in authority, called "the bishop" and "the
presbytery." As these form a choir or harmonious unit, so the rest
of the community are exhorted to form a choir and, by their concord
and submission, join this symphony of praise. Plainly, then, Ignatius
regards these *men* or *persons* as what we would call "the rank and
file" (as the common soldiers in the army of Christ, in contrast with
their commanders), or *the people* or *the laity* contrasted with *the
clergy.* Ignatius, in other words, assumes the existence of two well-
defined groups (note the use of the definite article οἱ) in the Church.
See *Trall.* note 15.

¹⁶ The rendering "melodies" seems to be more in keeping with the context than "members."

¹⁷ The adjective πνευματικός shares all the senses of the corresponding noun. See note 6. For the expression, "symphony of unity," 2 Cor. 6. 15 may be compared.

¹⁸ John 6. 33.

¹⁹ Cf. Matt. 18. 19, 20.

²⁰ Prov. 3. 34; James 4. 6; 1 Peter 5. 5.

²¹ A bishop's quiet and retiring manner (see Philad. 1) should not encourage taking advantage of it. He represents "the Master of the household." One should "fear" or "reverence" him.

²² The syntax of this sentence is not clear. I supply ἀκούετε after ἐπεί. For emendations of the text, see Lightfoot.

²³ See notes 6 and 17.

²⁴ "Born and unborn"; or "begotten and unbegotten." Christ was "born" in His human nature, "unborn" in His divine essence. Ignatius wrote before the Nicene Creed fixed the terminology more accurately: "genitus, non factus." Correctly understood, the words "created and uncreate" could also be applied to Christ. The expression "sprung from Mary" is another thrust at Docetism. See notes 1, 45, and 49.

²⁵ The Greek word means literally "filth," "scum," "offscouring"; it was a term used "of those criminals, generally the vilest of their class, whose blood was shed to expiate the sins of the nation" (Lightfoot). See Jer. 22. 28; Tob. 5. 20; 1 Cor. 4. 13 ("We are the world's refuse"). All that Ignatius seems to mean is: "I devote my life to you"; "I offer myself as a ransom for you"; or, perhaps, "I am the meanest among you"; "I am your lowliest servant." See 18. 1, and note 52.

²⁶ See Rom. 8. 5 and 8, and notes 6, 17, and 23. Other renderings would be: "to live the life of nature" and "to live the life of the Spirit."

²⁷ Regarding the word "Christ-bearer": F. J. Dölger, "Christophoros als Ehrentitel für Martyrer und Heilige im christlichen Altertum," Antike und Christentum 4 (1933) 73-80, has pointed out in reference to the present passage, that evidently Ignatius reminds his addressees of the pagan festivals held in honor of Artemis, "the Great Goddess of Ephesus." On these occasions miniatures of her great temple, also containing her image, were carried in solemn procession. Besides, pilgrims to famous shrines of a deity, such as, for example, Artemis, could purchase tiny reproductions of the shrine visited, to

be cherished as souvenirs or worn as amulets (cf. also Lightfoot's observations). In what sense the Christian Ephesians are to "bear" God, a temple, etc., Ignatius has intimated a few lines before: "you considered yourselves stones of the Father's temple . . ." This is only one of the numerous instances in which the early Christians availed themselves of the pagan terminology in use among their contemporaries and infused a new content into them. Note, incidentally, that Ignatius refers to himself in all his letters as "also called Theophorus." See note 2 of the Introduction and *Smyrn.* note 22; also Clement, note 68.

[28] 1 Thess. 5. 17. The quotation in § 2 is from Col. 1. 23.

[29] See notes 6, 17, 23, and 26.

[30] See Matt. 3. 7.

[31] Ephesus was "the highway of God's martyrs." Bands of prisoners from the East—including many Christians—intended for the shows and hunting scenes in the amphitheatre, would naturally pass through Ephesus, before taking ship for Rome (see Srawley). Note the words εἰς θεόν, victims "intended for God," that is, to be martyred for the sake of Christ.

[32] The word "eucharist" is quite general, but here doubtless refers to the celebration of "the Eucharist." See *Philad.* 4. The word "God's" should also be supplied with "praise." Cf. P. Batiffol, *L'Eucharistie, La présence réelle et la transsubstantiation* (9th ed. Paris 1930) 39-50. Since in the Koine the comparative often replaces a superlative, the words rendered "more frequently" may mean: "as frequently as possible."—In the following, Ignatius recommends concord and frequent eucharistic gatherings as a safe means of undoing the machinations of the enemies of the Church, whether these are "the forces of wickedness on high" (Eph. 6. 12), or earthly powers.

[33] 1 Tim. 1. 5.

[34] Faith and love (Ignatius hardly ever speaks of faith alone; see *Smyrn.* note 1) "are God,"—one of those pregnant expressions so frequently met with in the Fathers. If we possess faith and love in perfect blending, we possess God. One may recall Rom. 13. 10; 1 Tim. 4. 12; and, especially, 1 John 4. 8: "God is love."

[35] 1 John 3. 5; 5. 18.

[36] Matt. 12. 33.

[37] The Greek word δύναμις denotes power, faculty, capacity; also function, potency, and even action (e. g., the *action* of medicines);

similarly, not only " power to work miracles," but also " miraculous deed," " miracle."

³⁸ Ps. 32. 9; 148. 5.

³⁹ Eph. 3. 17; 1 Cor. 3. 16; 6. 19.

⁴⁰ 1 Cor. 6. 9, 10; Eph. 5. 5. The phrase " do not be deceived " or " do not let yourselves be led astray " recurs like a refrain in all the admonitions of Ignatius. The solemn warning, first sounded by Christ (Matt. 24. 4; Mark 13. 5; Luke 21. 8), was caught up by St. Paul, and is reiterated by the Apostolic Fathers. To us this constant warning against false doctrine is a guarantee that no false doctrine entered the infant Church. This reflection made a lasting impression on John Henry Newman and had a decisive influence on molding his future. See *Magn.* note 26 and *Pol.* note 12. See note 6 of the Introduction.

⁴¹ 1 Cor. 2. 6, 8.

⁴² The " unbelievers " here are evidently the Jews and Judaizing Christians, 1 Cor. 1. 23.

⁴³ 1 Cor. 1. 19, 20; Rom. 3. 27.

⁴⁴ John 7. 42; Rom. 1. 3.

⁴⁵ Another reference to Docetism. See notes 1 and 49.

⁴⁶ The words " in stillness " are variously interpreted. They may mean that these mysteries were wrought in God's " quiet way "; but while this would be true of the conception and birth of Jesus, it is not true of " the death of the Lord." Ignatius seems to mean that these mysteries were " accomplished," that is, that God's decrees concerning them were made, " in the stillness of eternity." The noun rendered " loudly proclaimed " recalls our expression " crying," as in " a crying need," a need that calls for notice. In this sense the three mysteries " were forced upon the notice of all the world " inasmuch as they were " loudly proclaimed " by the preaching of the Apostles.

Ignatius, it should be added, is the first writer outside the New Testament to mention the Virgin Birth. The deception of the devil in the economy of the Redemption became a favorite theme of the Fathers.

⁴⁷ Rom. 6. 4.

⁴⁸ For an explanation of the expression οἱ κατ' ἄνδρα, see note 15. Here it is used in a less stringent sense: " your entire community," " you all as one man," " you all, man for man."

⁴⁹ Rom. 1. 3. See note 45.

⁵⁰ 1 Cor. 16. 17.

⁵¹ Cf. T. Schermann, " Zur Erklärung der Stelle Epistula ad

Ephesios 20. 2 des Ignatius von Antiochien φάρμακον ἀθανασίας,"
Theol. Quartalschr. 92 (1910) 6 ff. J. R. Gasquet (*Studies* [West-
minster 1904] 259. 2) quotes one of the earlier editors, Wm. Jacobson,
as comparing the present passage with the *immortalitatis alimonia*
of the Post Communion of the 21st Sunday after Pentecost.

⁵² As a ransom for you "; this phrase has also been rendered (and
perhaps correctly): " Dearer to me than my own life are you." The
noun ἀντίψυχον (ransom) occurs again in *Smyrn.* 10. 2; *Pol.* 2. 3;
6. 1. See the use of περίψημα above in 8. 1 and 18. 1, and note 25.

⁵³ 1 Tim. 1. 1.

TO THE MAGNESIANS

The preceding letter to the Ephesians gives the reader a good
insight into the peculiarly Ignatian type of letter writing: it acquaints
him with the writer's general religious outlook; it puts him in possession of practically all the facts that seemed important to him; it shows
him what to expect, as he goes from letter to letter, in the way of
motivation for leading a truly Christian life. In each of the letters,
however, Ignatius managed to surprise the reader by a sudden flash
or two that diversify the general picture and supplied the addressees
with a fresh stimulus for accepting his exhortations. Thus the
Magnesians are told that submissiveness to ecclesiastical authority is
simply called for by the fact of their being " Christians"; and on
investigation we find that Ignatius is the first writer, in our extant
literature, to use the words " Christian " and " Christianity " as titles
of honor! The Smyrnaeans are exhorted to the same virtue on the
ground that its practice is the only means of being members of " the
Catholic Church "; and this, again, is the first occurrence of the
term in the ancient Christian writers! In the *Magnesians*, too, it is a
surprise to see how warmly Ignatius speaks of the Prophets—" those
men so near to God "; but a little reflection shows the appropriateness
of his admiration for them as a motive for definitely breaking with
Judaism. And did not St. Matthew designedly build up his Gospel
to prove the truth of Christ's message by insisting that He fulfilled
the ancient prophecies? And so there are flashes of light in every
letter which break its general tone. To discover these will be the
reader's own delight and privilege.

¹ In this brief address Ignatius finds room for twice mentioning

"God the Father" and "Jesus Christ"; for which see the Introduction, p. 53. St. Paul's greetings to the Churches had set the precedent, as, for instance, in Rom. 1. 7: "Grace to you and peace from God our Father and the Lord Jesus Christ." Another noteworthy feature is Ignatius's use of the preposition ἐν, "in" (see the Introduction, p. 58). It occurs six times in four lines! Like St. Paul, Ignatius views all manifestations of Christian life as those of a life lived "*in* God," "*in (union with)* Jesus Christ." This fact shows that the early Christians had a profound understanding of the Mystical Body of Christ. Cf. E. Mersch, *Le corps Mystique du Christ* (Louvain 1933) 234-44. Of course, once St. Paul had set the example, the use of "in" was natural and spontaneous to later writers even in contexts where the idea of this mystical union is not indeed lost sight of, but still kept somewhat in the background, as, for instance, in the expression "*through* Jesus Christ" above. See notes 13 and 30.

² Their love was "well-ordered" because they were "submissive to authority." Clement, in writing to the Corinthians, laments the lack of "good order" in that community as destructive of a truly Christian life.

⁸ The Greek genitive may be objective, "the faith in Jesus Christ," or subjective, "the faith given by Jesus Christ."

⁴ A reminiscence, no doubt, of St. Paul's "the prisoner of Christ Jesus," as in Eph. 3. 1.

⁵ The expression "flesh and spirit" occurs more than 40 times in these letters against Docetism. See notes 33 and 38, and *Smyrn.* same idea differently. See *Ephes.* notes 6 and 17. In the Church we have the *whole* Christ, His flesh and spirit, His body and soul, His human nature and divinity. This is one of the many warnings in these letters against Docetism. See notes 33 and 38, and *Smyrn.* note 5.

⁶ The antecedent of the pronoun ἧς is uncertain.

⁷ Does Ignatius mean the union "*of* Jesus *with* the Father" or our union "*with* Jesus *and* the Father"? Perhaps both senses are meant to blend. See note 3.

⁸ In the use of the verb τυγχάνω (see *Rom.* note 5) there is a hint of chance or uncertainty implied in the noun τύχη. Ignatius remembers St. Paul's exhortation: "Work out your salvation with fear and trembling" (Phil. 2. 12).

⁹ For the use of the terms "bishop," "presbyter," "deacon" (note that representatives of all three orders of the ministry had come from Magnesia to meet the bishop of Antioch!) see especially H. de

Genouillac, *L'Église chrétienne au temps de saint Ignace d'Antioche* (Paris 1907) 137 ff. See also *Philad.* note 12.

[10] This affectionate reference to deacons, even of Churches other than his own, occurs repeatedly in Ignatius's epistles. See *Ephes.* note 8 and *Philad.* note 11. Zotion may have proved helpful to Ignatius in various ways. He evidently wants him to stay with him.

[11] The bishop is here thought of as the dispenser of " God's grace," the presbyters as enforcing " the law of Jesus Christ." There is, evidently, a reference to the sacraments in the former expression, and one to preaching in the latter.

[12] The bishop's youth is " evident," " apparent " (perhaps " only too apparent ") and strikes the eyes of the body, while his authority is visible only to " the eye of faith " (see below, 6. 1).

[13] " Wise in God " is one of those numerous biblical or patristic expressions that have found their way into our everyday speech. Compare 1 Cor. 4. 10: " We are fools for Christ's sake, but you are wise in Christ." In not a few instances of Ignatius's use of " in " the modern mind finds it difficult to see eye to eye with him.

[14] For the verb θέλω, compare Matt. 27. 43. God " was pleased with us," that is, has deigned to choose us from the rest of mankind.

[15] " A human being ": here a rendering of the Greek σάρξ. See above, note 5, and *Ephes.* notes 6 and 17.

[15a] The followers of Christ called themselves " brethren," " saints," " believers," and " disciples." The word " Christian " appears in Acts 11. 26, 26. 28, and 1 Peter 4. 16. In Acts 11. 26 Luke reports: " At Antioch the disciples were for the first time called Christians." It seems that the pagans at Antioch coined the name " Christians " as from the proper name " Christ," just as they spoke of " Herodiani," " Marciani," etc. To them, therefore, " Christians " simply meant adherents of a man called Christ. Since the name originated at Antioch, it is not surprising that Ignatius of Antioch is the only Apostolic Father who uses it. Moreover, he is the oldest writer in early Christian literature to use both " Christian " and " Christianity " as titles of honor: *Ephes.* 11. 12; *Magn.* 4. 3; 10. 1, 3; *Trall.* 6. 1; *Rom.* 3. 2, 3; *Philad.* 6. 1; *Pol.* 7. 3. Tacitus (*Ann.* 15. 44) in his description of the fire of Rome uses the noun *Chrestiani*, but gives the name of the Lord correctly as *Christus*. In Pliny the Younger, a contemporary, we find the word *Christiani* seven times. For further details see K. Bauer, *Antiochien in der ältesten Kirchengeschichte* (Tübingen 1919); H. Dieckmann, *Antiochien ein Mittelpunkt urchristlicher Missionstätigkeit* (Aachen 1920) 30 ff.

[16] Attendance at regular (βεβαίως) church meetings and services authorized (κατ' ἐντολήν) by the bishop is often inculcated in these letters as the mark of a conscientious Christian.

[17] This expression is used by way of euphemism in a rather odious context in Acts 1. 25. On the use of "the accommodated sense" in quoting Scripture texts, see *Smyrn.* note 25. For an exceptional meaning of τόπος, see *Rom.* note 2.

[18] The Greek has "to die *into* the Passion." Through baptism "we died *into* His death," as St. Paul says in Rom. 6. 4; that is, we were "incorporated with Him." See also Gal. 3. 27 and above, note 1.

[19] The Greek word rendered "preside," here and in 2, distinctly implies *power* and *authority to command*. See *Rom.* note 2. Some texts read τύπον for τόπον.

[20] "At last"; "in these last days"; "at the end of the present age"; cf. Heb. 1. 2; 9. 26; 1 Cor. 10. 11.

[21] That is, "by outward appearances"; "after an earthly fashion." See note 15, and compare John 8. 15.

[22] John 5. 19 and 30; 8. 28. Note, incidentally, Ignatius's acquaintance even with the fourth Gospel, which was written only fifteen or twenty years before.

[23] The reference seems to be to doctrines hatched out in private conventicles.

[24] See Eph. 4. 3-6. "That," summing up the preceding clause, "is the whole, the true, the genuine Jesus Christ." Christ is not truly ours, and we are not truly Christians, unless we have "one prayer, etc."

[25] John 8. 42; 13. 3; 16. 28. With Ignatius's striking "assertion of the true divinity of Jesus during the incarnation" J. Moffatt, "Ignatius of Antioch. A Study in Personal Religion," *Journ. of Rel.* 10 (1930) 174. 9, appositely compares the lines by St. Thomas Aquinas:

> *Verbum supernum prodiens,*
> *Nec Patris linquens dexteram.*

[26] This important warning, first uttered by Christ (Luke 21. 8; Mark 13. 5), has since been re-echoed by the Church throughout the centuries. See 1 Cor. 6. 9; 1 Tim. 1. 3; Titus 1. 14; 3. 9. Warning against heresy is a mark of the true Church. While its frequent occurrence in early patristic times is a sad testimony to the constant dangers threatening from heretical teaching—a danger to which many individual Christians and even whole communities succumbed—it

is at the same time a guarantee to us that the Church was ever jealously watching over the *depositum fidei*. Gal. 1. 8; 1 Cor. 11. 2. See *Ephes*. note 40.

27 The edifying life of these holy men was actually (and, we may assume, also consciously) "in accordance with Christ's way" and patterned after Him. Without knowing the program He was to unfold centuries later, they actually followed it. They announced His coming, they waited for Him, they hoped in Him, and many of them were persecuted for His sake. And since they were saved, and salvation is possible only through the grace of Christ, they were actually saved by Him. Their teachings were incorporated in the Gospel, for Christ did not come to annul, but to fulfill, the Law and the Prophets. It is touching to hear Ignatius speak so warmly of these Prophets, calling them "most godly men."

28 This is a truly majestic reference to the Incarnation—the Word of God stepping forth from the silence of eternity! See *Ephes*. note 46.

29 "By a name other than this," namely, "Christian," which is understood after the mention (in the Greek) of "Christianity." Such inaccuracies or forms of brachylogy are common in Greek. See *Trall*. note 26.

30 "Be salted *by* Him"; "Let Him be your salt." But the Greek is more vigorous: "Be salted (and, as it were, soaked) *in* Him." See note 1.

31 Phil. 2. 11.

32 "One who is of less account than you are," "who is your inferior"; in other words, "who is not your superior or bishop."

33 Another warning against Docetism.

34 1 Tim. 1. 1.

35 Prov. 18. 17.

36 Ps. 1. 3.

37 The bishop is supposed to sit in the centre, surrounded by his presbytery. The word "crown" recalls the Latin *corona*, an encircling attendance. The men who made up this group were "fittingly selected," "appropriately chosen," for their task. All worked together, all were of one mind!

38 "In the flesh," that is, in His human nature. See notes 5 and 33.

39 As land is soaked with water, so these Christians were "absorbed or steeped in God." Not only were their minds continually occupied with God, but their whole way of life was divine; they were "full of God."

40 For "unflinching," see *Trall*. note 5 and *Ephes*. note 13.

TO THE TRALLIANS

No two Ignatian letters are alike, but, naturally, they bear a strong resemblance. They were written at the same time (some from Smyrna, others from Troas), under the same mental strain of the approaching martyrdom, and with the same religious fervor. Ignatius's master passion, his unbounded love for Christ, can see but one danger threatening the Asiatic Churches: the wiles of heretical teachers. Hence Docetism is a standing topic in all the letters; but here, as in those addressed to the Ephesians and Philadelphians, it seemed important enough to find a place even in the inscription. We may reasonably conjecture that these communities were particularly exposed to Docetic propaganda. But in this respect, as in some others, we must confess our ignorance. Unfortunately, too, Ignatius's diction is not always clear. In this epistle, for example, καθαρός has been suspected of being " some sectarian nickname (like our " Puritan "), for Ignatius never uses the term elsewhere of persons." In general, therefore, the reader of Ignatius may be warned that certain expressions well known to us from ancient Greek may yet have acquired in Hellenistic times some connotation, some local color, as it were, that escapes us.

It is a surprise to see that J. Moffatt, in " An Approach to Ignatius," *Harv. Theol. Rev.* 29 (1936), 9 f., though convinced that "in some real sense, which Ignatius does not define, the eucharist denotes sacrifice," explains θυσιαστήριον in 7. 2 " metaphorically, as the Christian congregation or People of God duly gathered for worship under its appointed clergy; it is the inner precinct of the Christian Altar, where the Lord imparts the substance and the vital energy of the gospel to true Christians . . . very much as the writer to the Hebrews could say that we Christians ἔχομεν θυσιαστήριον (13. 10) of our own." The same writer sees " Gnostic affinities " everywhere in Ignatius's language and finds him " naive " in his constant insistence on obedience to the clergy as the one means of salvation. See the same writer's otherwise appreciative inquiry, " Ignatius of Antioch, a Study in Personal Religion," *Harv. Theol. Rev.* 10 (1930) 169-86.

[1] The Trallians seem to have enjoyed freedom from persecution and from internal dissension; hence " internal and external peace." For the antithesis between " flesh " and " spirit," see *Ephes.* notes 6 and 17.

[2] Terseness in the use of prepositions is a marked, and often vexing,

feature of Ignatian style. " When we meet Him at the resurrection ":
literally, " at the resurrection toward Him." This recalls *Rom*. 2. 2:
" that I may *rise* in (*into*) His presence."

³ " In Apostolic fashion ": or, since Ignatius follows the precedent
set by the Apostles, "holding to the Apostolic tradition." See
2 Cor. 1. 2.

⁴ The word πλήρωμα, consecrated by St. Paul to signify *God's*
fullness, seems here to denote the fullness of grace. See, however,
Ignatius, *Ephes. inscr.*

⁵ For the adjective "unshaken," see *Ephes*. note 13 and *Magn.*
note 40. The precise sense of the words rendered " an acquired
habit " is not quite clear; they may, perhaps, mean "for occasional
use," as opposed to " ingrained habit."

⁶ Note the Pauline use of the preposition " in," so common in
these letters. See *Magn*. note 1.

⁷ Another Pauline touch is the expression "imitators of God."
See 1 Cor. 4. 16; 11. 1; Eph. 5. 1 and *Ephes*. note 3. The idea of
being someone's " imitator " was widely accepted in ancient life and
literature, and a Christian could readily transmute it into " following
in someone's footsteps." We, too, speak indiscriminately of " The
Following of Christ " and the *Imitatio Christi*. Cf. T. Preiss, " La
mystique de l'imitation . . ." (*Ephes*. note 3).

⁸ For κατὰ ἄνθρωπον—according to human standards, in a human
way, living the ordinary life of men—see Rom. 3. 5. The standards
in this case are those of unregenerate nature. See *Rom*. note 26.

⁹ That is, without authorization from the bishop, without his
consent, independently of him. See note 27.

¹⁰ 1 Tim. 1. 1.

¹¹ Literally, " living in whom we shall be found." The verb
rendered " to be found " need not mean, as it sometimes does, " to be
found " (that is, after investigation or, at death), but, in a more
diluted sense, " to be," much like the French *se trouver*, or the
German *sich befinden*. Moreover, the Greek future occasionally ex-
presses " expectation "; hence, here, " in (with) whom we are expected
to live," if we wish to be saved; " with whom we are expected to
live forever."

¹² For this expression, see 1 Cor. 4. 1. It is not clear whether the
word for " deacon " should here be pressed to mean what we mean by
its use, as in ch. 3. For ἀρέσκειν, see 1 Cor. 10. 33: the clergy must
give no just cause for complaint.

¹⁸ The text here is not certain.

[14] The Greek word means "band." Compare the German *Bund*. Several expressions both in Clement's epistle to the Corinthians and in the Ignatian letters seem to indicate that "the presbytery" ordinarily acted as a collective body. Cf. K. Prümm, *Christentum als Neuheitserlebnis* (Freiburg i. Br. 1939) 323.

[15] As Christ and His Apostles were a definite and distinctive group, so, Ignatius says, in a church deserving of the name there must be one group of persons (bishop, presbyters, deacons) sharply set off against another. See *Ephes.* notes 15 and 48; also note 36 below.

[16] The usual rendering "I think many things in God" seems meaningless. See the Introd. p. 58.

[17] Generally rendered "who would puff me up." Ignatius's friends would no doubt refer to him as a martyr, a confessor of the faith, etc.

[18] See Ignatius's letter to the Romans, which reads like a rapturous expression of his longing for the crown of martyrdom, or, as he puts it, for "perfect discipleship." See *Ephes.* notes 4 and 11.

[19] The words "of the honor" are implied in the context.

[20] Note the strong expression πολεμεῖ. Ignatius longed to suffer, but refused to think of himself as a hero, a martyr, a true disciple; hence there was a struggle, a war, going on his breast. His passionate desire for martyrdom "kept tugging at his heart," "put him on the rack."

[21] John 12. 31; 14. 30; 1 Cor. 2. 6, 8.

[22] 1 Cor. 3. 1, 2.

[23] "Pardon me": supply "if I refrain from speaking of heavenly things."

[24] Col. 1. 16.

[25] The sense seems to be: many things have yet to be done by us if we do not wish to miss, or "come short of," reaching God. The one great thing yet to be accomplished by Ignatius was to die for Christ.

[26] "Heretics": most translators say "they," though Ignatius has not spoken of any persons. For a Greek it was easy to pass from heretical *teaching* to heretical *teachers*. See *Magn.* note 29. The very παρεμπλέκουσιν means: "they weave (plait, braid) Jesus Christ into themselves," that is, "into their own web." There is here a mixing of metaphors, since the next sentence speaks of liquids.

[27] "Apart from": see note 9.

[28] On this use of "flesh" and "blood" see the observations by Lightfoot.

[29] Isa. 52. 5, freely quoted.

[30] Another warning against Docetism. See *Ephes.* note 24.

[31] Well explained by Lightfoot: "My life and my preaching alike are a falsehood against Him, for they assume that Christ really did rise." If the Docetists were right, Ignatius's testimony was false: "my life is a lie about the Lord."

[32] Matt. 15. 13.

[33] The Greek word rendered "means" often signifies "to promise," but since Ignatius here does not refer to a promise of something future, but declares (professes) a present fact, the rendering given in the text is preferable. God and we *are* one, as the head and the members are meant to be.

[34] The text is not certain.

[35] For "*the love* of the Smyrnaeans" see *Rom.* note 2.

[36] The reference is evidently to "the people" in their mutual relations, as distinct from their duty to their superiors. See *Ephes.* notes 15 and 48; also note 15 above.

TO THE ROMANS

This is the last of the four letters which Ignatius on his journey from Antioch wrote from Smyrna, where St. Polycarp was bishop. It may well be imagined that the farther westward he travelled, the more his mind was occupied with the scenes that would await him in the Amphitheatre, and the more his heart would throb with the prospect of at last becoming a true disciple of Christ. It is easy to believe, also, that the conversations of the two martyr saints were chiefly concerned with martyrdom both as a duty and a privilege of a Christian. But there was a tiny cloud looming on the Western horizon. Might not the Roman Christians, some of whom were prominent in public life, use their influence and obtain for him a stay of the capital sentence or even its complete revocation? Such a calamity must be prevented! And so, Ignatius resolved to write to the Romans, not to strengthen them in the faith, as he did the Asiatic Churches, but to beg them not to intervene in his behalf through "unseasonable kindness." There are passages in this letter, which portrays his love for Christ and his desire to die for Him, that have no equal in Christian literature. In fact, it is perhaps by this letter that Ignatius is best remembered by posterity. For depth of feeling and nobility of sentiment, a sentence like this is unforgettable: "God's wheat I am, and I am to be ground that I may prove Christ's pure bread." Cf. O. Perler, "Ignatius von Antiochien und die römische Christengemeinde," *Divus Thomas* 22 (1944) 413-51.

[1] See *Smyrn. inscr.* and *Philad. inscr.*

[2] Clear as the general theme of this letter is, its verbal expression teems with puzzles. This is especially true of the inscription.

"Through": more literally, "in accordance with," "conformably to." The following genitives may be objective ("faith in, and love for, Christ") or subjective ("faith and love imparted by Christ"). The Greek word τόπος often denotes a place or thing in one way or another distinguished; hence, "in the chief place of the Roman territory." But what does Ignatius mean by "the Roman territory"? What is its extent? There the Church "presides"; but how does she preside? Politically, culturally, morally, spiritually? There is no answer. Ignatius tells us where the Church presides, but fails to tell us "over what" she holds the presidency. The addressees understood, of course. Of the following six adjectives, each beginning with ἀξιο-, the sense is fairly clear, though "worthy of sanctification" is a puzzle. The adjective ἀγνός often means sexual purity. And shall we read χριστόνομος or χριστονόμος? The former would mean "governed by the law of Christ," the latter "keeping (maintaining, following) the law of Christ." Surely, to the Romans it was not doubtful what Ignatius meant to say. Other puzzles are pointed out in note 3.

But the real *crux interpretum* is the expression rendered "presiding in love." The word ἀγάπη is, of course, capable of several different senses; but why is it prefaced by the definite article? Some scholars are of the opinion that the puzzles of the inscription can be solved by assuming that Ignatius is alluding to the primacy of the bishop of Rome. See, for example, J. R. Gasquet, *Studies* (Westminster 1904) 248-81: "Lightfoot's St. Ignatius and the Roman Primacy." This is not the place to rehearse the argument for and against such an acceptation, and it is enough to say that the true meaning of the celebrated phrase is still an open question. One thing is certain: Ignatius is extraordinarily lavish in his praise of the Roman Church, and it is hardly admissible to assume that his encomium was no more than a *captatio benevolentiae* designed to wring from the Romans the favor he was pleading for. See J. Thiele, "Vorrang in der Liebe," *Theologie und Glaube* 19 (1927) 701-9; A. Ehrhard, *Die Kirche der Märtyrer* (Munich 1932) 276; O. Perler, *loc. cit.*; L. Kösters, *Die Kirche unseres Glaubens* (2d ed., Freiburg i. Br. 1935) 120; K. Bihlmeyer, *Kirchengeschichte* 1 (10th ed., Paderborn 1936) 102.

⁸ "In flesh and spirit": see *Ephes.* notes 6 and 17. In what sense had the Roman Church "every foreign stain thoroughly filtered out of it"? Errors of doctrine? Or errors of life? Perhaps the reference is to the Neronian and Domitian persecutions which may have acted like "a purge" of the Roman community.

⁴ Cf. Rom. 1. 9 ff.

⁵ For the Greek word rendered "obtain," see *Magn.* note 8. The adjective "due" renders the preposition ἀπο-.

⁶ It has been conjectured that "your love (charity, affection)" should in this context be substituted by "you who are united by Christian charity," "your brotherhood," "your community." The same has been said concerning other passages in these letters: cf., e. g., H. de Genouillac, *L'Église au temps de saint Ignace d'Antioche* 126, 238.

⁷ 1 Thess. 2. 4; Gal. 1. 10.

⁸ As T. Zahn suggests (*Ignatii et Polycarpi epistulae, martyria, fragmenta* [Patrum apostolicorum opera 2, 3d ed., Leipzig 1876] 59), this seems to be an allusion to the habit of craftsmen to inscribe their names on the completed work.

⁹ That is, "I shall become a martyr and thus proclaim the glory of God."

¹⁰ Compare Phil. 2. 17 and 2 Tim. 4. 6.

¹¹ Note this passionate outcry at the prospect before him: "How glorious it is to be a setting sun! May I be a sun that rises in His presence!" A ἵνα-clause may, of course, express a wish or command (cf. Eph. 5. 33). See note 18.

¹² In other words, "be consistent and practice what you are wont to inculcate in teaching disciples," the chief lesson being that a disciple must be ready to die for Christ. It is not clear whom Ignatius means in saying "you have taught *others.*" One may see in the adjective a reference to Clement, the bishop of Rome, who about twenty years earlier had written a letter to the rebellious community of Corinth.

¹³ "A believer": literally, "faithful," "loyal," that is, to Christ. Ignatius seems to say: "After my death I shall be spoken of as having been a true believer."

¹⁴ The convincing power of Christianity is not so much in what its defenders may say about it, as in its inherent greatness, which cannot fail to make an impression on outsiders. Christianity wins more adherents by the life of the faithful than by a discussion of its merits.

10¹

[15] 1 Cor. 9. 1; 7. 22.

[16] 1 Cor. 4. 4.

[17] Col. 1. 16. The Greek word rendered " fascinate " means to woo, court, try to obtain one's consent, attract, coax by admiring and praising.

[18] The Greek allows this clause to be taken as a wish: " Only let me make my way to God." See note 11. The early Christians were convinced that sufferings endured by martyrs are the work of the devil, that martyrdom is actually a conflict with the devil. Cf. F. J. Dölger, " Der Kampf mit dem Aegypter in der Perpetua-Vision. Das Martyrium als Kampf mit dem Teufel," Antike und Christentum 3 (1932) 177-88. This view is evident throughout the correspondence and treatises of St. Cyprian: cf. E. H. Hummel, The Concept of Martyrdom according to St. Cyprian of Carthage (The Catholic University of America Studies in Christian Antiquity 9, Washington 1946) ch. 3.

[19] Note this echo of Matt. 16. 26.

[20] 1 Cor. 9. 15.

[21] Literally, " Suffer me to copy the Passion of my God." The sentiment expressed in the preceding sentence is at first sight strange: " Once arrived in the pure light of the beatific vision, I shall be a man," that is, he shall have reached the perfection of human nature. In the present economy of salvation man is not " man " in the full sense of the word until he reaches his eternal salvation.

[22] I follow Origen's interpretation of this passage: Comm. in Cant. Cant. prol. (GCS, Origenes 8. 71 Baehrens). Lightfoot and others understand ὁ ἐμὸς ἔρως as " my earthly passions."

[23] John 4. 10; 7. 38.

[24] John 6. 33.

[25] John 7. 42; Rom. 1. 3.

[26] Such expressions as κατὰ ἄνθρωπον and κατὰ σάρκα are familiar from the New Testament. See Ephes. notes 6′ and 17, and Trall. note 8.

[27] See note 6.

[28] Here, as in Philad. 11. 2 and Smyrn. 12. 1, the preposition διά refers not to the scribe so much as to the bearer of the letter.

[29] 2 Thess. 3. 5.

TO THE PHILADELPHIANS

Among the Ignatian letters, this address to the Philadelphians gives the fullest résumé of the writer's Christian belief. Facts, moral exhortations, and mystical experience are thrown into one grammatical structure of unusual length, which rivals the address to the Romans. Note this ringing indictment of Docetism: the Philadelphian community " unwaveringly exults in the Passion of our Lord, firmly believes in His Resurrection," and is saluted by Ignatius " in the Blood of Jesus Christ." See *Trall.* prefatory note. Cf. M. Rackl, *Die Christologie des hl. Ignatius von Antiochien* (Freiburg i. Br. 1914). Philadelphia had been visited in person by Ignatius.

¹ Gal. 1. 1.

² " I am charmed," and not: " I am amazed (astounded, marvel)." The compounds of πλήσσω are capable of a more pleasant sense than that which our " amazement " conveys. See, for instance, Luke 2. 48: " they were overjoyed."

³ The word γνώμη connotes both understanding (thought, intelligence) and will (disposition, inclination, etc.). Ignatius lauds the bishop's " disposition to please God," " his Godward aspirations." See *Ephes.* note 13.

⁴ For this expression, see John 6. 57; Acts 14. 15.

⁵ Or "native to the light of truth," in Knox's translation (Eph. 5. 8).

⁶ John 10. 7 ff.; Matt. 7. 15.

⁷ Gal. 5. 7; 1 Cor. 9. 24-26.

⁸ Matt. 15. 13.

⁹ 1 Cor. 6. 1 and 10; see *Ephes.* note 40.

¹⁰ 1 Cor. 10. 16 and 17.

¹¹ In Christian antiquity places of worship contained one altar, and one only. The significance of this fact is explained by F. J. Dölger, " Die Heiligkeit das Altars und ihre Begründung im christlichen Altertum," *Antike und Christentum* 2 (1930) 183. For the expression "my fellow servants," see 11. 1; also *Ephes.* note 8 and *Magn.* note 10.

¹² Ignatius never tires of laying his finger on the hierarchical constitution of the Church. The function which by Christ's institution belonged to the distinct group called " the Apostles " passed on in due time to another distinct group called " the presbyters of the Church." Clement, too, insists on the need of this " Apostolic succession " in Church government. The Gospel is called " the flesh of

Jesus" because it is the record of His earthly life, etc. In the first
and the second century the term "presbyters" often included bishops.
See *Magn.* note 9.

[13] 1 Tim. 1. 1.

[14] Matt. 23. 27.

[15] 2 Cor. 11. 9; 12. 16; 1 Thess. 2. 7, 9.

[16] John 3. 8.

[17] 1 Cor. 2. 10 and 11; 14. 24 and 25. For the following, compare
the incident related in Acts 12. 20 ff., of a delegation of Tyrians and
Sidonians applauding a speech by Agrippa I with the cry, "It is the
voice of a god, not of a man." See especially F. J. Dölger, ΘΕΟΥ
ΦΩΝΗ. Die Gottes-Stimme bei Ignatius von Antiochien, Kelsos und
Origenes," *Antike und Christentum* 5 (1936) 218-23.

[18] Matt. 16. 17.

[19] Eph. 5. 1; John 8. 38.

[20] John 8. 32.

[21] The reference is, evidently, to the ancient authoritative records
(as it were, "the archives") of the Old Testament, as opposed to
the New. The Greek here is extremely condensed: "If I do not find
(this or that) in the Old Testament, I do not believe it at all; for I
do not believe in the Gospel."

[22] John 10. 7 and 9.

[23] Literally, "all these things." In Greek a general neuter expression often designates persons, as, for example, in John 6. 37. It is
here all the more natural because ταῦτα πάντα includes *things*, since
"the Church" implies all the means of sanctification (sacraments,
etc.); similarly, "the Prophets" implies their prophecies, etc. But
the sentence as a whole is somewhat vague, since the verb is omitted.
Another puzzle is the expression "the oneness of (or, with) God,"
for which compare "the oneness of Jesus Christ" above in 5. 2.
The sense seems fairly clear: no matter what means God has devised,
whether in the past or in the present, they all have but one purpose
(εἰς)—to unite us with God; in this way all these things are "one in
(with) God." As many tributary rivers "empty into" the main
stream, so "all these things" are means of uniting us with God.

[24] Phil. 1. 8. The word σπλάγχνα means "tenderness," "affection,"
"compassion," or simply "heart." See Philem. 7, 12, 20; 1 John
3. 17; Col. 3. 12.

[25] "The Name": frequently used absolutely in early Christian
literature for "the name of the Lord Jesus." See *Ephes.* note 10.

[26] See *Rom.* note 6.

[27] 1 Tim. 1. 1.

TO THE SMYRNAEANS

The address to the Smyrnaeans is short, but affectionate. Ignatius is now at Troas, and the end of the journey is not too far distant. Of the three letters written here, two are intended for Smyrna. He doubtless never forgot all that he had seen and heard and experienced in Polycarp's episcopal city: the people overflowed with faith and love, were endowed with every gift, lacking in nothing, radiant with God's splendor. And then there were reminiscences of a more personal nature. His trip to Smyrna had been a *via* made *dolorosa* by ten leopards in human form; but there came a respite at Smyrna, and the Churches of Asia vied with each other to comfort him " in flesh and spirit." A special letter of thanks was due to the Smyrnaeans. But Ignatius is always true to himself. The inroads of heresy weigh heavily on his mind. So the first part of the letter is devoted to an attack on Docetism, not by argumentation, but by triumphantly pointing out fact after fact of Christ's life and redemptive work. There follows one of his favorite exhortations: follow the presbytery, follow the Apostles, follow Christ, as He followed the Father. If you do this, he says, you will be members of the Catholic, the universal, Church. In conclusion he asks the Smyrnaeans to send a delegation to Antioch, where the Christian community was again enjoying peace.

[1] Note the ever-recurring formula " faith and love " in the Ignatian letters (see *Ephes.* note 34) and, indeed, in the Apostolic Fathers. The nature of this " love " is briefly described in 6. 2; compare also Clement 8. 4. See St. Paul's eulogy of love in 1 Cor. 13. 4-13.

[2] The same praise was accorded by St. Paul to the Corinthians; see 1 Cor. 1. 7. For χάρισμα, " gift," " grace," in the wider and the narrower sense, see F. Zorell, *Lexicon Graecum Novi Testamenti* (2d ed., Paris 1931) *s. v.*; for the literature, cf. I. Rohr, " Charismen," *Lex. f. Theol. u. Kirche* 2 (1931) 838-40.

[3] The precise meaning of ἁγιοφόρος is not clear; but see *Ephes.* note 27. If the word means " bearer of sacred vessels," the sacred vessels which the Church of Smyrna bears are the Christian graces and virtues (Lightfoot). The rendering given in the text is a possible alternative.

[4] Cf. M. H. Shepherd, " Smyrna in the Ignatian Letters," *Jour. of Rel.* 20 (1940) 141-59.

[5] Literally, " in flesh and in spirit." See *Ephes.* note 6 and *Magn.* note 5; also notes 6 and 8 below.

⁶ Rom. 1. 3 and 4. One of the many attacks, in this letter and elsewhere, on Docetism. See the Introduction, note 7.

Matt. 3. 15. See note 25.

⁸ "Really," "truly," not merely "in appearance." See notes 6 and 12. This entire ch. 1 reads like a Creed. Note, too, that Ignatius is nowhere *proving* the doctrines he lays down or arguing in a theological fashion: *his* proof is the clear statement of facts that were handed down from the Apostles and are based upon the Scriptures. The pronoun "whose" in the next sentence refers either to "Christ" or to "the Cross."

⁹ Isa. 5. 26; 11. 12; etc.

¹⁰ All men, Jews and Gentiles, are united "in a single body, that is, His Church." See the note (29) on "the Catholic Church." Ignatius's language recalls that of St. Paul's letter to the Ephesians, which contains the classic texts for the "oneness," the ἓν σῶμα, of the Church; for example, 1. 23; 2. 16. The expression "of *His* Church" recalls Christ's reference to "*my* Church" in Matt. 16. 18, and to "*my* sheep" in John 21. 16 ff. Compare also John 10. 16, "one flock, one shepherd." Cf. C. C. Richardson, "The Church in Ignatius of Antioch," *Jour. of Rel.* 17 (1937) 428-43.

¹¹ Christ "raised Himself from the dead" or "was raised by the Father." For the former expression, compare John 10. 18.

¹² To judge from Ignatius's persistent condemnation of Docetism, the danger threatening the early Church in Asia from that heresy must have been grave and ever-present. See K. Bihlmeyer, *Kirchengeschichte* I (10th ed., Paderborn 1936) sections 11. 1; 28. 2; 29. 2.

¹³ Since these heretics denied the Resurrection of Christ, they could not expect to share in the glorious resurrection of their own bodies.

¹⁴ Luke 24. 30-43.

¹⁵ Acts 10. 41.

¹⁶ "Spiritually": that is, in His divine nature and in His "spiritualized" or glorified body and soul. See note 5.

¹⁷ Here, as frequently in these letters, Ignatius recommends the prayer of intercession. He seems to suppose that the entire community, headed by the bishop and the presbyters, joins in this prayer. Cf. Matt. 18. 19 and 20. We know from the Acts how fervently the Christians would give themselves to prayer to obtain some favor or to avert some calamity from an individual or the community. See Acts 4. 24 ff.; 12. 15. Also note the reference to prayer as a means of

obtaining the grace of conversion: ἵνα μετανοήσωσιν. See Clement, ch. 7 f. and note 35.

[18] Rom. 8. 17.

[19] Not "the perfect man," since the article τοῦ belongs to the participle. Another thrust at Docetism. See notes 8 and 12. Compare the Athanasian Creed: "Perfectus Deus, perfectus homo: ex anima rationali et humana carne subsistens."

[20] A reminiscence of Phil. 4. 13.

[21] For the sense of the phrase οἱ κατ᾽ ἄνδρα, see Ephes. notes 15 and 48.

[22] A σαρκοφόρος, as opposed to a νεκροφόρος, is, evidently, a person of real and living flesh and blood. See note 3.

[23] For the significance of this repeated warning, see Ephes. note 40 and Magn. note 26. Cf. 1 Cor. 6. 9.

[24] Col. 1. 16.

[25] Matt. 19. 12. The Fathers felt quite free in quoting Scripture texts out of their natural context and making use of what is called "the accommodated sense." The practice of the Roman Liturgy is the same. See Magn. note 17.

[26] The word τόπος is well explained by Lightfoot in his note on Pol. 1. It means: high rank, office, dignity, place of honor or authority. This sense may have a bearing on its use in the Rom. inscr. See Pol. note 4.

[27] The statement that "the Eucharist is the flesh of Jesus Christ" recalls Luke 22. 19. According to Tertullian (Adv. Marc. 4. 40 [CSEL 47. 560 Kroymann]), the Docetist Marcion denied this truth. Cf. A. Scheiwiler, Die Elemente der Eucharistie in den ersten drei Jahrhunderten (Mainz 1903) 17-26.

[28] John 4. 10.

[29] This is the earliest occurrence in Christian literature of the expression "the Catholic Church." "Catholic" means, of course, "universal," as opposed to "individual," "particular." The context in which it appears elucidates its meaning. Ignatius is convinced that in the Church the presbytery follows the Apostles, just as the Apostles followed Jesus Christ, and as Jesus Christ followed the Father. "I count you happy," he says (Ephes. 5. 1), "who are so closely knit to him as the Church is to Jesus Christ, and as Jesus Christ is to the Father." Drop a link in this chain—people, presbytery, bishop, Apostles, Jesus Christ, the Father—and, Ignatius argues, there is no Catholic Church. See Philad. 3. 2. This "following" or "union," according to Ignatius, has to do both with doctrine and

government. He believed, therefore, in the monarchical constitution
of the Church, in her Apostolic succession, in her orthodoxy. To him
the term "Catholic Church" conveyed the same meaning as at the
present day. Some fifty years or so later, the author of *the Martyrdom
of Polycarp* uses the same expression: see the *inscr.*; also 8. 1 and
16. 2. The first of these passages speaks of "all the παροικίαι
(stranger-groups; parishes; dioceses) of the holy and Catholic Church
in every place." In 16. 2, Polycarp is called outright "the bishop of
the Catholic Church in Smyrna." The value of this latter testimony
has been called in question for the reason that the Moscow MS. (see
Lightfoot's note) substitutes "holy" for "Catholic." Later, in the
third century, the word *Catholica* could be used alone for *Ecclesia
Catholica*; cf. O. Rottmanner, "Catholica," *Rev. Bénédictine* 17
(1900) 1-9.

[80] The name *agape* (generally rendered *love feast*) was given to
meals prepared from offerings by the faithful and taken to the
accompaniment of prayer and song. Their purpose was to express
the unity and fraternal love of the members of the Church. Cf. K.
Völker, *Mysterium und Agape. Die gemeinsamen Mahlzeiten in der
alten Kirche* (Gotha 1927).

[81] Heb. 6. 19.

[82] 2 Tim. 1. 16.

[83] The word σωματεῖον was sometimes used in the sense of "body
corporate." After the persecution the Church at Antioch had, as it
were, recovered its "own bodily condition," the condition belonging
to a church "when in normal health." The immediate reference,
however, seems to be to its normal growth and full complement.

[84] Literally, "the affection of the brethren." This makes sense; but
see *Rom.* note 6.

[85] It seems that young women or virgins were at that time allowed
to join the class of "widows" and devote themselves to works of
charity. Cf. T. Schermann, *Die allgemeine Kirchenordnuung des
zweiten Jahrhunderts* (Paderborn 1914) 1. 202 ff.: "Die christliche
Jungfrau und Witwe."

TO POLYCARP

This is the last, as it is the shortest, of the Ignatian epistles, written like the preceding at Troas and sent to Smyrna. But this is a personal letter; its addressee is bishop Polycarp, although a portion of it is concerned with " you," the community. Here, then, bishop speaks to bishop, an old man to one his junior by many decades. Whether the two men had ever met before Ignatius's visit to Smyrna we cannot tell. At all events, the tone we know so well from the rest of his correspondence is the same: direct, straightforward, and even blunt, as when he urges Polycarp: " Beg for an increase in understanding! " Friend or no friend, Polycarp must be warned of the dangers of the times and told what his duties are. After all, both serve the same Master: God the Father and the Lord Jesus Christ. But all this freedom of speech is mellowed by an undertone of cordiality which, toward the end, bursts into the unusually solemn address: " My dear God-blessed Polycarp! " Perhaps this last portion will linger longest in the mind of the reader. Ignatius, taking for granted, as well he might, that all the Churches in Asia form a sort of supra-diocesan community, a supra-racial unit in Christ, tells Polycarp that it is fitting to convene a council invested with all the splendor of God, for the purpose of electing a man to be God's courier and hasten to Antioch and deliver the greetings of the sister Church of Smyrna on the occasion of tranquillity restored to that community. What a spectacle of Christian solidarity!

Here, as elsewhere in his letters, Ignatius is not prodigal of words. He is a foe to verbiage. It would be difficult anywhere to pick out even a small number of words that can be spared. It follows, then, that recourse to the Greek original is a goal worthy of any reader's earnest endeavors. Written without literary aim or ambition, the Ignatian letters are the records of a human heart molded by the love of Christ.

[1] The noun ἐπίσκοπος (including one instance of the abstract noun ἐπισκοπή and two examples of the verb ἐπισκοπεῖν) occurs no less than 55 times in the seven Ignatian letters. Their total number in the New Testament is only 12. To take them out of these epistles would be to take the heart out of them; for around them cluster his most earnest exhortations to the Asiatic Churches. It is also significant for Ignatius's concept of Church government that the same word is

used for God and man, man being the visible head of the Church on earth, God the invisible Head in heaven.

[2] The opening word "I am well pleased" strikes a cheerful note at the outset. It means "to welcome, approve, think favorably of, admire." It occurs also in *Ephes.* 1 and in *Trall.* 1. "Your God-mindedness": more literally, "Your mind (fixed upon, absorbed in, united with) God." Ignatius's subtle power to do wonders with the preposition ἐν has often been referred to in these notes. Compared with his terse and telling expressions, English is poorly equipped for dealing with the doctrine of the Mystical Body of Christ.

[3] Literally, "to add to your race," that is, "to increase its speed and vigor." Polycarp lived up to this counsel of his friend by ending his career with martyrdom. Metaphors from the racecourse, describing the life of a Christian, are common in the Fathers since St. Paul's use of them (2 Tim. 4. 7; 1 Cor. 9. 24-26). See below, 6. 1 and *Ephes.* note 12; also Clement, note 25.

[4] Note τόπος in the sense of "dignity, office," and compare *Rom.* note 2. For the much-used antithesis of "flesh and spirit," see *Smyrn.* note 5.

[5] See Gal. 6. 2 and Eph. 4. 2.

[6] The rendering "to each one singly" does not seem to do full justice to the Greek. See *Ephes.* notes 15 and 48. Ignatius exhorts Polycarp to imitate God's accustomed way (that is, His gentleness, forbearance) in speaking to the people, the *laity*. Ecclesiastical superiors should not only exact obedience from their subjects, but also treat them with due charity. See note 9.

[7] Matt. 8. 17; Isa. 53. 4.

[8] It seems best to retain the word "athlete" for "combatant," "fighter," "wrestler," as applied to a Christian. See note 3; also Clement, note 25. Compare the present letter, 2. 3 and 3. 1. A kindred thought is expressed by Job (7. 1) in the familiar saying: "*Militia* est vita hominis super terram."

[9] Luke 6. 32. In the following, again stress is laid on the need of πραότης in dealing with inferiors: gentleness, forbearance, long-suffering. The noun recalls the beatitude: "Blessed are the gentle (πραεῖς), for they will inherit the land" (Matt. 5. 5). There is a touch of humor in Ignatius's prescribing "wet applications" for "hot fevers."

[10] Matt. 10. 16.

[11] The text here is assumed to be corrupt. The translation adopted seems, however, to give Ignatius's thought. "Be on the alert" is the

warning sounded by the aged bishop—"read the signs of the times."
See 3. 2.

[12] 1 Tim. 1. 3 and 6. 3, where, too, bishop speaks to bishop.
Through all the Apostolic Fathers runs the warning cry: μὴ πλανᾶσθε.
It is a guarantee of the purity of their doctrine.

[13] Widows, orphans, and slaves (see § 3) have always been objects
of special care on the part of ecclesiastics. The care for "the poor"
is a sign of a Christlike attitude. Note, too, the homely as well as
practical counsel of pastoral theology: "Seek out all (members of
your parish or diocese) by name." Since the comparative in the
Koine may do duty both for an emphatic positive and for a mild
superlative, a rendering like "frequently" or "rather frequently"
may be substituted for "as frequently as possible" in the next paragraph. See the comparative in John 13. 27.

[14] The meaning of κακοτεχνία is not obvious. The translation given
assumes that Ignatius refers to slaves scheming to be set free. Perhaps, however, there is a reference to the schismatical designs of false
teachers, as most editors think.

[15] Ignatius is ringing the changes on his favorite antithesis between
"flesh and spirit." See note 4.

[16] Eph. 5. 25-29.

[17] The Greek defies exact reproduction: "If anyone can *remain*
continent, let him *remain* also in unboastfulness." Persons pledged
to continence should *steadily* or *stubbornly* refuse to yield to the
temptation of boasting about it.

[18] The translation given makes sense; but the meaning intended
may, perhaps, be: "If he thinks of himself more highly than of the
bishop" who, it is supposed, is a married man. Again, the subject of
γνωσθῇ may be the person's *vow* of chastity: "if *it* is better known,
more talked about, than the bishop." For ἐν ἁγνείᾳ, compare Matt.
19. 12.

[19] Titus 1. 7; 1 Cor. 4. 1.

[20] 2 Tim. 2. 4; Eph. 6. 11-17; 1 Thess. 5. 8.

[21] It is interesting to note Ignatius's use of the Latin terms *deposita*
and *accepta*. On this Zahn (see *Rom.* note 8) makes the apposite
observation that without doubt Ignatius had heard the words often
enough as used by the ten Roman soldiers who guarded him on his
long journey. A soldier received only a part of his pay at stated times;
the rest was deposited for him (*deposita*) in a savings-bank attached
to the cohort and paid out in cash or land (*accepta*) when he
received his discharge.

²² The word θέλημα generally refers to God's will (see *Rom.* I. I; Clement 20. 4); here, however, it may mean no more than an "order" from the emperor or some other official.

²³ The current translations of ἔμπροσθεν are too artificial to be correct: "in front of," "on the hither side," that is, in the context, "this side and *nearer to Syria* than to Churches beyond Antioch"! The adverb, when not further qualified, is used in the sense of "preferred"; hence "principal, chief."

²⁴ Some render "the wife."

INDEX

INDEX

Aaron, 12, 36
Abel, 11
Abiron, 12
Abraham, 14 f., 20, 28, 88, 107, 110
accepta, 145
accommodated sense, 141
Adam, 13, 40, 127
ἀδελφότης, 105
adultery, 27, 31
adversary, devil, 40
agape, 93, 113, 134, 142
Agathopus, Rheus, 89, 93
ἁγιοφόρος, 139
Agios O Theos, 110
ἁγνός, 134
Agrippa I, 138
Alce, 95
alms, 113
altar, one, 7, 71, 86, 137; cf. also 112
amphitheatre, 54, 123, 133
amulets, 123
Ananias, 37
angels, 27, 30, 31, 76, 92
animal world, 22
antidote against death, the Eucharist is, 68
ἀντίψυχον, ransom, 125
Antioch, 53, 54, 56, 89, 98, 127, 133, 139, 143, 146
Apollonius, presbyter, 69
Apollos, 38
Apostles, 3, 12, 34, 36, 38, 54, 57, 65, 73, 76, 77, 78, 82, 86, 88, 93, 124, 132, 137, 139, 141

"Apostolic fashion," 131
Apostolic Fathers, 3, 7, 103, 115, 124, 139, 145
Apostolic succession, 112, 137, 142
Apostolic tradition, 7
Arabia, 25
Ark, 14
arena, Christian life as, 13
Artemis, 109
Asia Minor, 53, 56, 57
Athanasian Creed, 78
athletes, 12, 105, 144; the master a., 96; Polycarp is God's a., 97
Atlantic Ocean, 109
Attalus, 99
Aurelius, Marcus, 108
authority, in Church, 5, 6, 7, 47, 125; origin of, 112; in Apostolic Fathers, 115; of Scripture, 113; of the state is from God, 116
Azarias, 37

babes, Trallian Christians so termed, 76
Babylon, 106
backbiting, 27, 31; see slander
baptism, 93, 98, 128; of Christ, 67, 90
Bardenhewer, O., 103, 118
Bardy, G., 109
Bareille, G., 118
Barnabas, St., 54, 103
Barnikol, E., 106
Bassus, presbyter, 69

149

καθαρός, 130
κακοτεχνία, 145
Kingdom, of God, 35, 42; of Christ, 40; see Christ, God
Knopf, R., 8, 105, 106, 108, 110
knowledge, divine, 33
Knox, R., 112
Koine, 123, 145
Korn, H., 119
Kösters, L., 134
Krüger, G., 8, 59

Laban, 28
Lactantius, 109
λαικός, 112
laity, 34, 112, 121, 144
Lake, K., 8, 59
last epoch, 64
law, observance of, 39
λειτουργία, 113
leopards, soldiers guarding Ignatius, 82, 139
Levites, 28, 34, 112
life, and immortality, 30; carnal, spiritual, 63; restoration to new, 60; in Christ, 64
light, 83; of truth, to be born of, 85
Lightfoot, J. B., 8, 55, 59, 118, 120, 122, 132, 142
Limbo Patrum, 115
Linus, St., 3, 115
liturgical gatherings, 103; see meetings
liturgical prayer, for the state, 116
liturgy, 7, 113; Roman, 104, 116, 141
λόγια, 108, 117
λόγος, 121
long-suffering, 17, 98; God's, 64

Lord's Day, 72
Lot, 15
love, 39f., 48, 60, 61, 67, 69, 71, 79, 81, 87, 92, 93, 98, 114, 142; in Christ, 114; well-ordered, 69, 126; of one's country, 43; of Roman Christians must not wrong Ignatius, 80ff.; see faith (faith and love)
love feast, 142; see agape
lying, God not capable of, 26

Macedonia, 56
macrocosm, 108
magic, 67
man, formed by God, 29
Marchal, L., 118
Marciani, 127
Marcion, 141
marriage, requires sanction of bishop, 98
Martial, Epigrams (7, 8, 16, 21), 106
Marty, J., 116
martyrs, 65, 106, 132, 135; Ephesus the highway of, 123; sufferings of, 136
martyrdom, concept of, 136; a conflict with the devil, ibid.; a setting of the sun, 81; duty of a Christian, 133; of Polycarp, 142
μαρτυρεῖν, 106
Mary, Christ's mother, 63, 77; a virgin who conceived Christ of the Holy Spirit, 67
μαθητεύειν, μαθητής, 121; see disciple, discipleship
Matthew, St., Gospel of, 125
mediatorship, of Christ, 104

unbelievers, 66, 76, 78, 91, 92, 124
understanding, 96
union with God; with Christ, 68, 114; of Christ with the Church, 111
unity, 30, 32, 61f., 65, 69, 80, 86, 88, 96, 142
universe, 26, 41, 83
Ussher, J., 55

viaticum, 105
Verbum supernum prodiens, 128
Virgin Birth, 67, 90, 124
virginity, 114
virgins, 95, 142
virtues, Christian, 139
vision, beatific, 136; of Perpetua, 136
vivere secundum naturam, 108
voice, man's as voice of God, 87, 138
votive offerings, 34
Vulgate, 104

war, 11
water, consecrated by Christ's Passion, 67; Living, 83
weeds, among Christians, 86; of the devil, 64

West, 106
Western boundary, 12
wheat, of God, 133
widows, 13, 92, 95, 97, 142, 145
windlass, faith a spiritual, 64
winds, 109
Wisdom, a collective title, 44, 116
witness, 117; see martyr
wives, Christian, 97; Christian at Corinth, 10
women, heroism of, 42; Christian, 106
Word, of God, 117; Christ, 72, 129; see Christ
workman, 29
works, a Christian's, 98
world, constitution of, 46; Christian detachment from, 104
worship, 48

youth, Christian, 23; the Christian at Corinth, 9f.
ὑποτάσσεσθαι, 115

Zahn, T., 55, 135, 145
zeal, 97
Zeller, F., 8, 59
Zizzamia, A. I., 112
Zorell, F., 139
Zotion, deacon, 127